Farm Fields

Cottonwood Grove

Cattail Marsh

Steep Banks

Pond

Island

Muskrat Lodge

Pond Places

To Michael. Remember snorkeling after
turtles in Burntside Lake?—Mom-Ann

The animals and plants illustrated in this book occur widely in ponds and marshes across
North America. Your pond may not have *all* these species, but it will probably have most of
them or their look-alikes. The selected species have been reviewed and approved by scientists
at the Denver Museum of Natural History.

We wish to thank Dr. Charles Preston, Curator of Ornithology at the Denver Museum of
Natural History, who checked this book for scientific accuracy. We also wish to thank
Dr. Michael J. Weissmann, Faculty Affiliate, Department of Bioagricultural Sciences and
Pest Management, Colorado State University, who reviewed the facts on insects.

Book design by Jill Soukup

Library of Congress Cataloging-in-Publication Data
Cooper, Ann (Ann C.)
        Around the pond / Ann Cooper ; illustrated by Dorothy Emerling.
            p.     cm. -- (Wild wonders series)
        Summary: Examines the interdependent lives of the various animals and plants that
inhabit various parts of a pond from the surface film of the water to its weedy depths.
        ISBN 1-57098-223-6 (pbk.)
        1. Pond animals--Juvenile literature.   [1. Pond animals.  2. Pond plants.
3. Pond ecology.  4. Ecology.]   I. Emerling, Dorothy, ill.  II. Title.  III. Series.
        QL146.3.C66  1998
        591.763'6--dc21
                                                                          98-25065
                                                                            CIP
                                                                            AC

Published by the Denver Museum of Natural History Press
2001 Colorado Boulevard, Denver, Colorado 80205  www.dmnh.org
in cooperation with Roberts Rinehart Publishers
6309 Monarch Park Place, Niwot, Colorado 80503
Tel. 303.652.2685  Fax 303.652.2689  www.robertsrinehart.com

Distributed in Ireland and the U.K. by Roberts Rinehart Publishers
Trinity House, Charleston Road, Dublin 6, Ireland
Distributed to the trade by Publishers Group West

Printed in Hong Kong

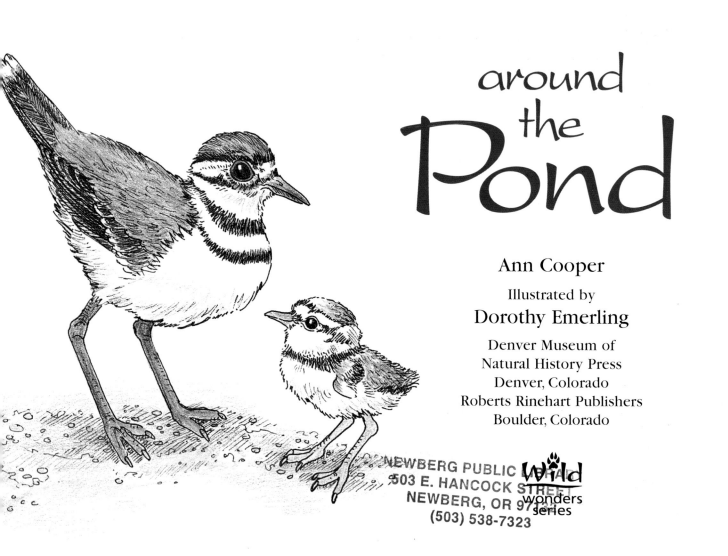

# around the
# Pond

Ann Cooper

Illustrated by
## Dorothy Emerling

Denver Museum of
Natural History Press
Denver, Colorado
Roberts Rinehart Publishers
Boulder, Colorado

Wild
wonders
series

# Spring Fever

Swirls of snow drift over farm fields and meadows. The pond lies locked in ice. The only sign of life is a lacy, paw-print trail from the woods to the marsh— until one sunny day, spring blows in on a warm wind. It wakes the pond, bringing begin-again fever.

Ducks become jittery. They chase across the pond, all skitter, splash, and quack. Long V's of geese fly in from the south, honking. They use their webbed feet as brakes. Splashdown! Small birds flit everywhere. The marsh is loud with twittering. The air is musky-damp. It smells of growing.

What makes the pond such a noisy, busy place?

A pond is full of hideaways: tangled waterweed jungles, dense cattails, muddy-buggy shorelines, fallen logs, lily pads, nest-safe islands, steep banks for dens, and shady trees. In water and on land, there are scores of places to live and raise a family.

Marshy edges and wet meadows nearby soak up rain and melting snow like a giant sponge. The moisture helps plants sprout. Water drains into the pond, carrying with it soil, minerals, and dead plants and animals. They act like pond vitamins, making nutritious pond "soup." On land and in water, pond habitats grow lots of food: roots and shoots, seeds and weeds, prey for predators, and especially insects galore.

No wonder so many creatures choose to live here!

# Froggy Went A-Courting

Bullfrog spent the winter at the bottom of the pond, not moving, not eating. His body was as cold as the mud in which he hid. As the spring sun warmed the pond, Bullfrog stirred from his muddy hideout. He kicked his chilly legs and swam slowly up, up.

For hours he sprawled in a tangle of pondweed near the surface, basking. He kept watch, his bulgy golden eyes just above the water, alert for danger. Until he was toasty, he could not swim fast, or leap far, or escape from hungry herons or raccoons.

Time passed. Bullfrog felt strong and fast, ready to go courting. One night he swam to his finest weed patch. *Bur-rum, bur-rum,* he croaked in his deep voice. All around him frog-songs rumbled and clicked in the steamy evening air. He called again, *Bur-rum,* trying to make his voice heard in the din.

At last! A female swam over and touched him, excited by his fine voice. He grabbed her from behind in a hug. She laid her jelly-eggs. As the eggs streamed out, Bullfrog fertilized them with his sperm so they would grow. He let go of this mate. *Bur-rum, bur-rum.* With his mighty voice, he would charm many mates tonight!

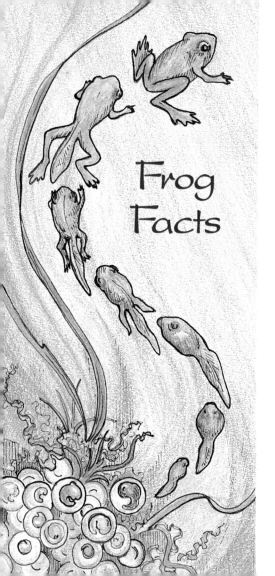

# Frog Facts

## Jelly-Eggs
Bullfrog females lay clusters of up to 20,000 eggs. In a week or so, the eggs hatch into wiggly-tailed tadpoles.

## Tadpole Tales
Bullfrog tadpoles eat algae (green slime). As they grow, their tails shrink, their legs sprout, and they become tiny frogs. The change takes two years.

## Breathing
Tadpoles breathe with gills, like fish. Frogs use their lungs, like people. Frogs also breathe through their moist skin.

## On the Menu
Most frogs eat insects, spiders, worms, and other small prey. They catch insects with a quick zap of their long tongues.

## Ears, Eyes, Nose
A frog's ears are flat circles, like drum skins, near its eyes. A frog's eyes and nostrils are high on its head. It can see and breathe when it is mostly underwater and hard for predators to see from above.

## Noise by Boys

Only male frogs call to attract mates. Chorus frogs make sounds like a fingernail scraping the teeth of a comb. Leopard frogs "snore." All scared frogs squawk or croak when they jump back into the pond.

## Snack Attack

Bullfrogs, the largest frogs in North America, eat mice, baby birds, lizards, snakes, fish, snails, and small frogs!

## Toad or Frog?

Toads and frogs are amphibians. They can live both on land and in water. Toads have warty skin. Frogs have slimy skin. Slimy skin stops a frog from drying out on land and makes the frog slippery for enemies to catch. Some frog slime has a bad taste. Some is even poisonous.

## Enemies

Herons, rats, snakes, raccoons, fish, turtles, mink, larger frogs, and some people eat adult frogs. Dragonfly larvae, water beetles, fish, newts, and birds eat tadpoles. Leeches and insects eat frog eggs.

# The Best Nest

Blackbird was so-o busy collecting leaves and grass to weave her nest. She had chosen a site in the marsh where the water was deep enough to keep her nest safe. She strung her nest between dead cattail stalks, weaving each strand tightly around the stems so the nest would not slip or tip. It was a strong, deep cup. She lined it with mud and bits of fine grass. After five days, her nest was ready.

She laid four blue eggs. For eleven days she kept them snug under her warm body. She left them only while she pecked a quick snack. At last, her chicks hatched. What scrawny, wobbly scraps they were—all beaks and squawk!

While Blackbird built her nest and incubated her eggs, her mate sat high on a cattail, squawking. *Kon-karee, kon-karee,* he called, lifting his wings and flashing his bright shoulder feathers. He was boss of this cattail patch, and his job was to make sure all the other blackbirds knew it! If other males flew into his space, he called, flashed, and chased them away. But when big birds—crows and hawks—flew by, he ganged up with the other male blackbirds to send the big birds off. That way, they could all keep their families safe.

# About Blackbirds

## Working Mom

A female blackbird's job doesn't end when her eggs hatch. She brings food for her chicks until they leave the nest. She carries their fecal sacs (poop) and drops them far from the nest to keep it clean.

## Oops!

Sometimes a hammock-nest tips when the stems that support it grow unevenly. Eggs topple out. Some chicks die when they fall out of the nest before they can fly. Snapping turtles or fish eat them.

## Neighbors

Wrens, song sparrows, and warblers also nest around the marsh.

## Looks

Male red-winged blackbirds are flashy so they can attract mates and show other males the space is taken. Females are drab and streaky so they won't give away their nest sites.

## Blackbird Rivals

In ponds and marshes in the West, yellow-headed blackbirds push the redwings out, taking the best waterfront nest sites.

## Enemies

Hawks, owls, and crows prey on blackbirds or their chicks. Foxes, mink, raccoons, and weasels take eggs and nestlings— if they can get to them. Water snakes slither up to nests, too.

## Food

Blackbirds eat all kinds of insects. Caterpillars and mayflies are favorites. They also eat all kinds of seeds.

## Winter

Blackbirds leave the pond in winter. They glean (gather) grain and weed seeds in fields and roost in noisy treetop flocks.

# Skunked

Dusk was falling, bats flitting, as Mother Skunk left her leaf-lined den below a fallen tree in the cottonwood grove. Her five playful youngsters followed in a line, staying close. This was their first outing. Outside was a scary place.

*Snuffle, sniffle, snuffle.* As she waddled along, Mother Skunk poked her pointy nose into the soil to sniff out beetles, worms, and other tasty food. The little ones copied her, poking and scrabbling. Their tiny noses twitched and quivered with excitement.

The smallest one, last in line, pounced on a beetle. The other youngsters scuttled back to have a look. *Crunch!* Smallest One ate the beetle before his litter mates could wrestle it away.

Mother Skunk ambled down a worn trail to the pond. She knew a good place to hunt for turtle eggs. As she came to the bank, she stopped short. A fox! Next-in-line Baby almost crashed into her.

Mother Skunk strutted toward Fox, her legs stiff. She lifted her tail high, showing off her elegant white stripes. She stamped her feet once, twice. Fox backed away from his duck-feast, his muzzle feathery. He knew that high-rise tail! He knew there was no enemy fiercer or smellier than a protective mother skunk. Phew! He had met that awful stink before.

# Skunk Snippets

## Warning!

Black and white are tip-off colors that remind enemies to leave skunks alone. If they don't, the skunk squirts its stinky spray as far as twelve feet, accurately! Spray stings the enemy's eyes and makes it feel sick and gag. The smell lasts for days.

The foul, oily liquid squirts from two marble-size glands near the skunk's tail.

Skunks try their spray against cars, too. Of course, it does not work! Many skunks become roadkill.

## Family Life

Skunks raise their five to nine babies in ground dens lined with grasses. The babies are mouse-size at birth. They can spray by two weeks old, even before their eyes open, even before they grow sharp teeth and thick, glossy fur.

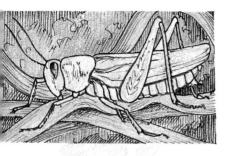

## Chow Time!

Skunks are omnivorous. They eat almost anything: grasshoppers, beetles, voles, mice, turtle eggs, fruit, grain, berries, and vegetables.

Skunks also eat the eggs of birds, such as ducks and coot, that nest on the ground. They crack open large eggs by throwing them back through their legs to hit a hard surface.

## Enemies

Skunks have such a good defense that few enemies seek them out. Eagles, coyotes, foxes, bobcats, and badgers sometimes eat them. Great horned owls hunt them more often. (Owls have a poor sense of smell.)

## Travelers

Skunks may travel far on the hunt. They bed down for a day's sleep wherever they happen to be—in brush piles, culverts, abandoned fox or coyote dens, hollow logs, even under people's porches.

## Tree Nests

Wood ducks nest in tree cavities. Their eggs are safe from skunks. When the chicks are ready to leave the nest, they take a giant leap!

# Little Monster

Dragonfly Nymph skulked in the waterweeds. He watched the mosquito wigglers hanging from the surface of the pond. Before, he would have feasted on them. Today he was not hungry. He did not even move when a plump tadpole wiggled by. His outside skeleton felt tight. It was time to shed one last skin, time to take to the air.

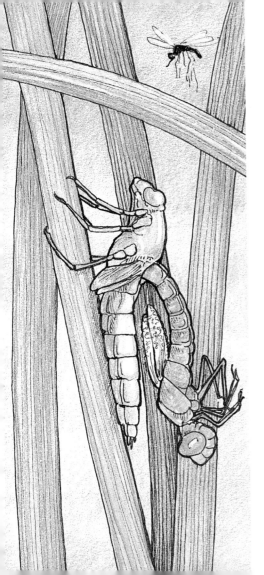

Claw by claw, he pulled himself up a bulrush stem. He kept climbing until he was well clear of the water and any hungry, jumping fish. Clinging with his six feet, he tensed his body muscles. His too-tight skin split along the back. Slowly, he struggled out of his old shell. At first his wings were milky-pale and crumpled. He pumped "blood" into his wing veins until the wings stiffened and spread.

For two hours he dangled from the remains of his old skin, waiting for his wings to harden. Zoom! He hurtled into the buggy air to hunt. He ate mosquitoes and midges in the air. But when he caught a moth, he zipped back to perch on a cattail. He clipped off the moth's wings and ate its soft body.

# Dragonfly Details

## What Big Eyes . . .

A dragonfly's eyes are so big they take up its whole head. The eyes are compound eyes. Each has thousands of seeing cells, or facets, which see a tiny part of the view. Together they see a complete picture.

## Exoskeleton

Outside skeletons do not stretch. A nymph sheds its hard skin every time it needs growing room. It may live in the water for 2 or more years and shed up to 15 times.

## Jet-propelled

Dragonfly nymphs take in water through their tails and breathe oxygen from it. They can also squirt the water out in a jet to scoot themselves away from predators.

## Dragon or Damsel?

A dragonfly perches with its wings out to the side. A damselfly folds its wings over its body.

## Fossil Record

Long before dinosaurs lived, huge dragonflies with two-foot wingspans flew in the swamps.

## Mating Time

A male dragonfly grabs the back of his female's head with his claspers. She curls her tail under his body to get sperm to make her eggs grow. The two often fly joined until the female lays her eggs in a plant stem, in wet wood, or in the pond.

## Flight Champions!

Dragonflies fly much faster than you could peddle your bicycle! They zip to and fro or hover like helicopters, moving their four wings independently.

## Eat . . .

A dragonfly is a fierce predator at all stages of its life. A nymph (larva) eats insects, tadpoles, and even small fish. It grabs prey by shooting out its spoonlike, bristle-tipped lower jaw. An adult dragonfly catches its insect prey in the air by forming its bristly legs into a basket.

## . . . Or Be Eaten

A dragonfly is also prey at all stages of its life. Water birds, snakes, frogs, turtles, fish, and big insects eat nymphs. Birds, frogs, and turtles catch dragonfly adults, especially newly hatched ones that cannot fly well yet.

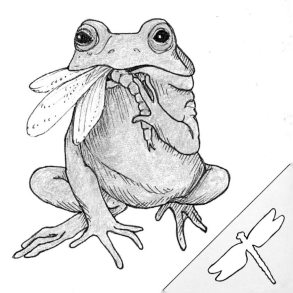

# Grab a Ride!

Mother Grebe was on nest duty when her chicks hatched. One by one, they pecked out of their eggshells. At first their downy feathers were spiky and damp. In the warm air, they soon dried. The chicks looked like little striped fuzz balls. Soon, they wanted food.

Mother Grebe clucked softly for her chicks to follow and slipped off her nest into the water. They bobbed in the water like tiny corks, but soon got the idea of swimming. Father Grebe fed one of them a small beetle he had caught. The other chicks fussed around, wanting some, too.

A shadow flickered over the pond. Mother Grebe watched, clucking her chicks close. A mother could not be too careful! It was a hawk gliding low over the marsh in search of mice or voles. Then she saw a mallard hustling her chicks out onto the island, quacking noisily. Something had bothered her. *Cluck-quick,* Mother Grebe seemed to say. Her chicks scrambled up on her back, and she ferried them quickly home to the nest. It was the safest place to be when a snapping turtle was on the prowl.

# About Grebes

## Nest

A pair of grebes builds a well-hidden floating nest—like a small private island—out of rushes and sedges. They anchor the nest to standing reeds.

## Eggs

A female pied-billed grebe usually lays from four to seven bluish eggs. Parents share sitting duty. The female takes longer turns. When she leaves, she covers the eggs to hide them.

## My Space!

Grebes guard an area around their nest site. It is their territory.

## Neighbors

Many ducks feed in the open water along with the grebes. Dabbling ducks, such as mallards, pintails, and teal, upend to feed. Then all you see are tails! They eat water plants and seeds, snails, leeches, worms, and insects.

## Splatter, Splash!

A grebe's legs are set far back on its body and its toes have lobes. This makes it a strong diver and swimmer. When it comes to flying, it is hard for the grebe to take off. It splashes for a long way across the water.

## Food

Grebes eat small fish, crayfish, dragonfly and damselfly larvae, water boatmen, snails, diving beetles, frogs, and some water plants.

## What a Voice!

Grebes are silent except at nesting time, when they call: *cuck, cuck, cuck, cow, cow, cow, cow-ah, cow-ah.* They sound spooky.

## Dabchick

The pied-billed grebe (in the story) is named for its two-colored beak, or bill. The bird is called water witch and dabchick, too.

## Going Down

Grebes dive well, even with young aboard! If a hawk threatens from above, a grebe flattens its feathers, squeezing out air that helps it float. It slowly sinks in the water.

# Turtle's Travels

Food was so-o easy to find in midsummer!
The pond seethed with insects, tadpoles, snails,
and little fish. In no time at all, Turtle had eaten
enough. Claws scrabbling, she scuffled onto a
slimy floating log and settled down to bask.
Only twice did she plop off her log—once
when a shadow-of-hawk passed, and again when
a short, sharp rain fell. She needed an all-day
siesta to rest up for her coming journey.

Late afternoon, Turtle headed for the shore. She swam past the water lilies, through a floating jungle of bladderwort and bur reed, into the shallows. What a tangle! She pushed by a clump of pickerelweed and plodded up the steep slope. On and on she trudged, not stopping until she reached a sandy bank on the edge of the fields. The soil was damp—good for digging.

Turtle dug with her hind claws, flicking soil back without looking. When her nest was smooth and about three inches deep, she laid six leathery eggs in it. With great care, she covered the eggs with soil and stomped it flat. She scuffled dead leaves and grasses over the diggings to disguise them. Her job of mothering was done.

# Turtle Tidbits

## On the Menu

Insects, tadpoles, snails, fish, cattail seeds and stems, algae (green slime), and even dead animals are part of a turtle's varied diet.

## No Teeth

Turtles tear their food with horny "beaks."

## Mobile Home

A turtle can't come out of its shell, which is part of the turtle's skeleton. The top shell has an outside layer of horny scales and an inside layer of bone, which is fused to flattened ribs.

## Short Stack?

Turtles can't make their own body heat. They bask in the sun to warm their bodies and strengthen their shells. Safe basking places—on logs, rocks, and muskrat or beaver lodges—may be in short supply. So the turtles clamber on top of one another.

## Long Rest

Turtles hibernate in mud at the bottom of the pond. It is warmer than the water! They cannot breathe with their lungs underwater. They get enough oxygen from the water through the skin of their mouths and throats.

## Ice Magic

Ice is lighter than water and floats. If this were not so, ponds would freeze from the bottom up. Fish, frogs, turtles, and pond insects could not survive.

## Predators

Skunks, foxes, raccoons, badgers, and ground squirrels dig up and eat turtle eggs. Wading birds, frogs, fish, and snakes eat hatchlings and young turtles.

## Marathon!

A newly hatched turtle's first task is to find water. It can be a long and dangerous journey. Scientists do not know for sure how turtles find the way. They might head for moonlight reflected in the pond.

# Waterweed Jungle

Diving Beetle lived among a tangle of weeds not far from the shore. Sometimes a water strider skittered by on its long legs, making shadowy dimples. Other times whirligigs near the lily pads swam tight circles in search of food. Mostly, this was a calm, quiet-seeming place. But down below, it was a jungle! And Diving Beetle was one of the fiercest hunters in it!

Many other kinds of beetles and bugs lived among the weeds. Tadpoles that looked like wiggly commas grazed the water plants for slime. Shoals of minnows darted through the weed forest, catching the light as they turned. Caddis fly larvae crawled along in their twiggy cases. Diving Beetle had his choice of prey. He scuttled through the weeds, using his back legs like tiny oars, and snatched a small tadpole to eat.

A hunting snake passed overhead, disturbing a mass of mosquito wigglers dangling from the surface by their tails—breathing. The wigglers sank down into the weeds. A giant water bug sped by, his back covered with his mate's eggs. Diving Beetle went on hunting. He had plenty of air trapped under his wing cases to stay down in his jungle for hours.

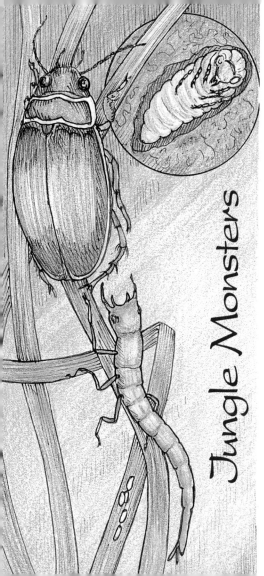

## Jungle Monsters

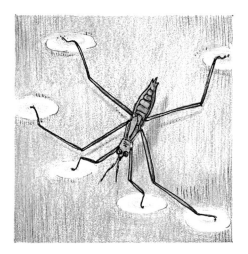

### Life Cycle

A diving beetle begins its life as an egg laid in a plant stem or in water. It hatches into a larva called a water tiger. The larva eats and eats and sheds its skin to grow. It crawls from the pond, burrows into moist soil, becomes a pupa, and at last hatches into a beetle.

### Skate Champions!

How can water striders skitter across the water without sinking? Their bristly feet spread their weight and trap small cushions of air that keep them from piercing the surface "skin" of the water.

### Whirligigs

Whirligig beetles glean hatching midges and other small insects from the water surface. Their spinning may help them "round up" prey. They have split eyes that see under and above water at the same time.

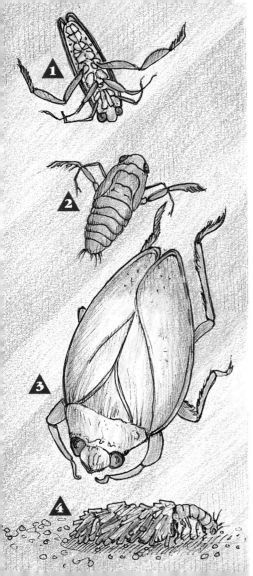

## More Insects

**1** Backswimmers swim upside down with jerky strokes using their bristle-fringed hind legs as oars.

**2** Water boatmen swim right side up and paddle with middle and hind legs.

**3** Giant water bugs are also called "toe biters." They eat tadpoles, fish, and insects. Some males carry their mate's eggs cemented to their backs to keep them safe.

**4** Caddis fly larvae glue tiny pebbles or twigs into cone-shaped, spiral "jackets" to protect their soft bodies.

## Snorkel Tail

A water scorpion looks a bit like a stick insect. It has a long, tail-like breathing tube. It pokes this "snorkel" through the surface film to breathe.

## Snails

Snails are part of the pond's cleanup crew. They scrape algae off leaves, stems, logs, and rocks, and eat it.

# Gone Fishing

Heron stretched his neck and ruffled his wings. He tweaked a feather into place with his beak. Dawn was painting the sky with pale golden streaks. It was time to go fishing! He flapped from his treetop perch. With slow, graceful wing beats, he soon arrived at his best fishing hole.

*Kok, kok, kok.* A harsh voice called from the cattails. Bother! A bittern was here first. Heron touched down on his lanky legs a little farther along the shore, startling a snipe that flew off with a harsh *skipe* call. Heron settled his wings and waded slowly, so-o slowly in the shallows, scarcely rippling the mirror-water. He stopped, statue-still, and watched for shimmery fish-flashes.

Jab! He thrust his beak deep into the weeds to snap up an unwary crayfish. Stab! He speared a bluegill. Bluegills were such finny fish! Heron dropped his catch for an instant. He snatched it up again, headfirst, so fish fins would not catch in his throat. Gulp! A bulge traveled down Heron's snaky neck as he swallowed. Yum! Good breakfast.

# About Herons

## Nests

Herons usually build straggly nests in treetop colonies with other herons. They find sticks on the ground or steal them from neighbors!

## Family Life

Male and female herons both care for eggs and chicks. Their three to four blue-green eggs hatch in about a month. Chicks are ungainly, scrawny, and always hungry. The parents throw up partly digested fish into the chicks' mouths. Later they dump whole fish into the nest and let the chicks fight over them.

## Beaks and Feet

A heron's beak is strong and sharp, great for stabbing slippery fish. Long-toed feet spread the heron's weight so it does not sink much into mud. Long legs allow the heron to wade in belly-deep water!

## Enemies

Crows and ravens eat herons' eggs. Eagles, red-tailed hawks, vultures, raccoons, and bears prey on nestlings. If a heron survives its first year, it can live more than twenty years.

## Food Fight?

Herons, kingfishers, grebes, and other birds all eat fish. You might think there would not be enough food for all of them.

Most of the time the birds avoid fighting over food by using different parts of the pond, catching prey in different ways, and hunting at different times of day.

## Something Fishy

Herons eat fish, frogs, toads, small turtles, voles, mice, baby birds, and insects.

## Fair Shares

Each kind of fish-eating bird has its own special fishing style. A heron stalks and jabs or "freezes" and stabs. A grebe dives from a swimming position. A kingfisher dives from its perch and catches small fish with its beak. It eats back at the perch.

# Muskrat's Morning

Muskrat lived in a stretch of the marsh between a cattail bed and a small island. This morning she planned to scent-mark some boundary places with musk to remind muskrat neighbors to keep out. But first, food! She gnawed a chunk of cattail stem and towed it to her nearest feeding platform. Scrabbling out of the water, she held the stem in her paws. She stripped away the tough outer leaves, nibbling only the juicy bits inside.

*Tsuk, tsuk.* A wren buzzed in alarm. Muskrat quit munching mid-mouthful. Was Fox prowling? Was Raccoon about? Home was not as safe as before.

After a hot summer, the pond had shrunk. The mud flats where the sandpipers foraged had dried and split into curly crusts. Muskrat could no longer reach her bank den from the water. The channel she had dug was high and dry. Too bad! It had been a cozy home for her and the babies, with its three chambers. Now she had to build a new house in deeper water for safety.

All morning Muskrat clipped and snipped, towed and tugged, piling cattails onto a mud mound. The pile grew. Soon she had the start of a fine lodge. She hollowed out a room inside, above waterline, and dug doors underwater for safe homecomings. Yes, this would be a good winter home!

# More About Muskrats

## Families

A mother muskrat gives birth to 4 to 7—sometimes up to 11—babies in a litter. Babies are born almost naked, helpless, and blind. After 2 weeks their eyes open. They can dive and swim. A female muskrat may have up to 5 litters a year. Wow!

## Neighbors

Many birds (especially ducks), snakes, snapping turtles, frogs, toads, and skunks may bask or snooze on muskrat houses or live inside them—even when the muskrats are there!

## Teeth

A muskrat's lips close behind its sharp, ratlike front teeth so it can gnaw plants underwater and not swallow water as well.

## Hungry, Hungry!

Left alone, some ponds fill with mud made from dead plants. Live plants start to grow far out in the water. In time, the pond becomes a marsh, then a meadow. Munching muskrats help keep the pond open. If *too many* muskrats are born, they eat so much that food runs out! The muskrats must move—even cross-country—to a new home.

## Enemies

Mink, hawks and owls, coyotes, foxes, weasels, dogs, raccoons, snakes, and snapping turtles prey on muskrats.

## Tales of Tails

Muskrats have scaly tails that are flattened side to side. They use their tails as rudders to steer when turning.

A beaver's tail is like a flat paddle. It helps the beaver balance on land when it is chomping trees. The tail is a fat store. Beavers warn other beavers of danger with a loud tail slap on the water. *Splash!* The sound carries far.

## Marsh Munchies

Muskrats are mainly plant eaters. They eat juicy roots, shoots, and stems of water plants. When plants are scarce they may eat fish, frogs, clams, crayfish, young birds, and carrion (dead animals). Beavers feast on tender aspen and willow bark.

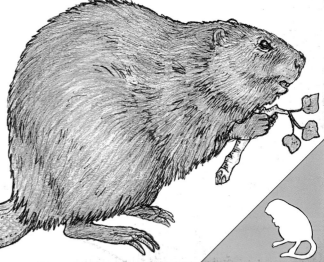

# Animals All Around

Each muddy bank, fallen snag, cattail marsh, and quiet bay shelters countless creatures. Anywhere you go, there are more animals around than you see. Here are others you might meet around a pond.

## Moose

These huge, gangly animals live in spacious areas in northern North America and the Rocky Mountains. They feed in woodlands and marshy ponds and lakes.

Moose are tall—more than six feet tall to their shoulders, not counting their heads and antlers! They could not fit through your front door.

## Milkweed Beetles

These beetles feed on poisonous milkweed plants that make them taste bad to birds. Their bright patterns warn birds to leave them be.

## Mosquitoes

We think of them as pests, but mosquito eggs, larvae, and adults are important links in the pond food chain.

## Snapping Turtles

"Snappers" like to rest in the mud, with only eyes and nostrils showing. They have huge heads and jaws. Besides eating plants, they eat insects, fish, young muskrats, and birds—often snapping up ducklings from below.

## Crayfish

These lobster look-alikes live in holes in muddy pond banks or under rocks. A tail-flick propels them backward to escape danger.

## River Otters

These sleek, playful mammals live in ponds and rivers where they have wildness and space.

## Did You Find?

Bear
Deer
Fox
Mink
Canada goose
Bittern
Hawk
Killdeer
Wren
Water snake
Chorus frog
Fish
Insects galore! (Ladybug, cricket, damselfly, mayfly, beetle, grasshopper, mosquitoes)

# Baby Boom

A pond habitat suits many animals, with its meadows, marsh, and open water, and all the busy edges in between. It is a great place to raise a family. Not all the young grow up in the same way.

▲ Some young hatch from fragile or leathery eggs. Whether they have feathers or plated shells, you can tell from the start what they will grow up to be.

▲ Some young are born live. They are furry, are fed milk, and look like small versions of their parents.

△ Other young look nothing like their parents. As larvae they live and act differently than adults.

Can you match △-adults with the correct △-young?

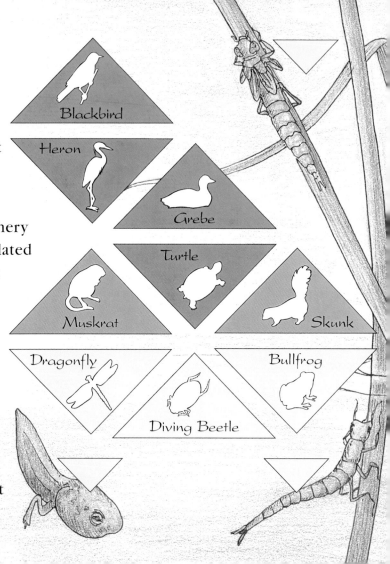

# TABLE of CONTENTS

# CHAPTER ONE

# INTRODUCING THE TAR HEEL STATE

Tourists flock to the beaches near Cape Hatteras Lighthouse, where you can find some of the best fishing and surfing on the east coast.

**North Carolina is a unique state for many reasons.** Although it's not a big state, more people live in North Carolina than in many other states. Also, forests grow near the coast because sand dunes block the spray of the ocean's harmful saltwater. Third, the state has some unusual wildlife, including rare fish and birds. Fourth, the state's climate is so changeable. Part of North Carolina may be subtropical, or very hot and humid, while another part may be as cold as southern Canada.

The state has two nicknames—the Tar Heel State and Old North State. The first nickname says a lot about the people of North Carolina. Southern Soldiers who refused to retreat during the Civil War were known as "tar heels." The nickname referred to the tar supposedly stuck to the soldiers' shoes. It became a badge of bravery. The tar was made from the state's once great forests of long-leaf pine. The second nickname sets North Carolina apart from the other Carolina to the south.

Since colonial days, North Carolina has played an important part in

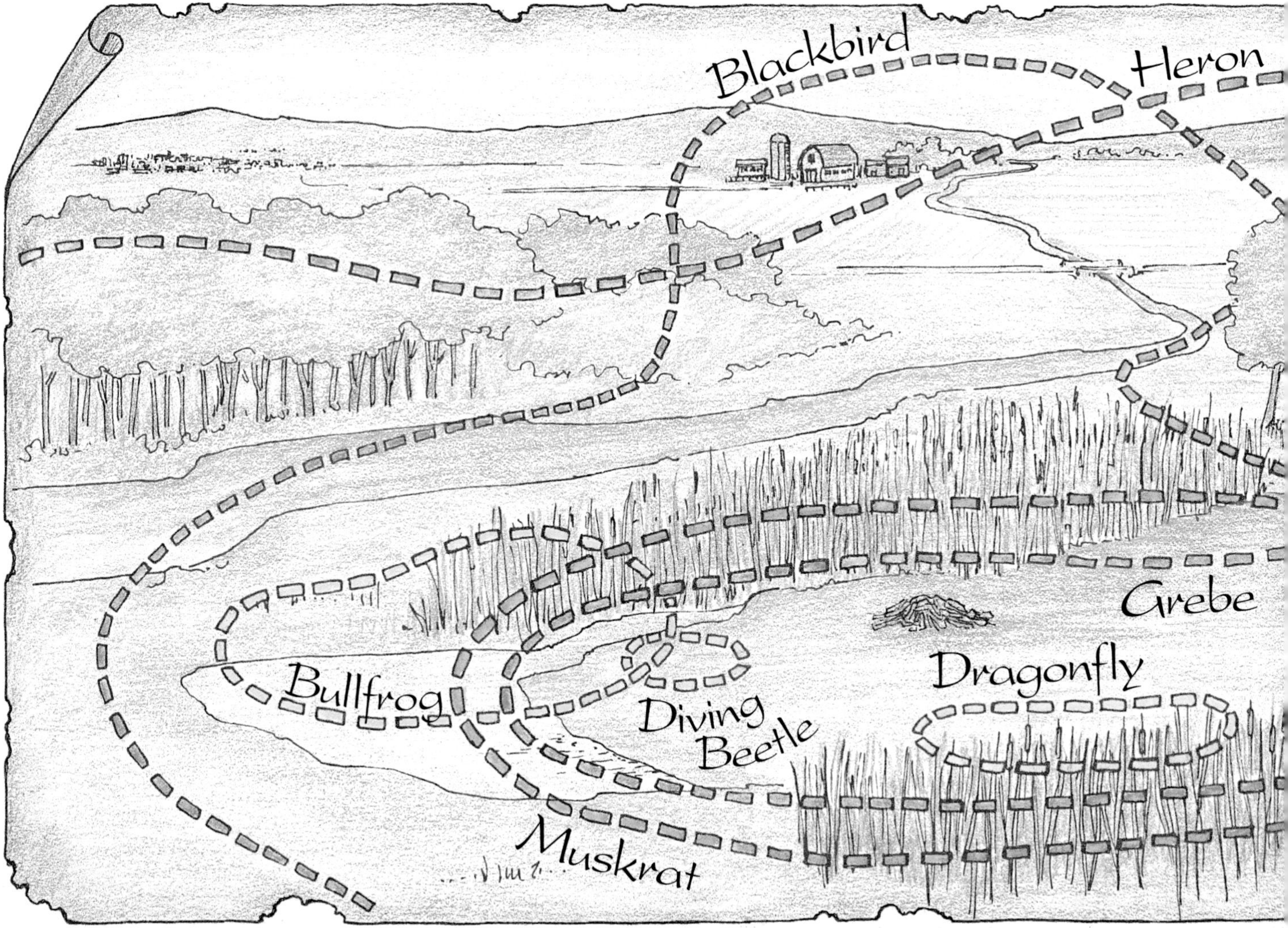
Blackbird
Heron
Grebe
Dragonfly
Bullfrog
Diving
Beetle
Muskrat

Year by year, the pond itself also changes. Water plants in and around the marsh shed leaves. The leaves slowly decay, making new soil on land, new mud in the water. The edges of the marsh become drier. Maybe trees and bushes grow. The pond gets shallower. In time, plants grow farther out in the pond or all the way across.

Years pass. What was once a pond and marsh becomes a tree-bordered meadow—unless floods come to scour the pond, unless muskrats munch cattails faster than they can grow back, unless beavers dam the river, making a new pond. Nature is not fixed. Change is natural.

Will your pond be different next year? There is only one way to find out!

# Links of Life

A breeze ruffles the bright yellow cottonwoods. Leaves swirl. Puffs of cattail seeds drift through the air like snow. There is a chill in the wind and a hint of winter. The pond is quieter now than it was in spring. No frogs call. No insects chirp. Few birds trill their sweet songs. What is happening?

Many summer birds have flown south. Insects to eat are in short supply. Frogs, toads, and turtles have settled into the mud underwater or underground. Fish, dragonfly larvae, and tadpoles hang out in the waterweed jungle, scarcely moving. As seasons change, animals' lives change in and around the pond.

## Tracks

Did you notice tracks or prints on some pages? They are life-size. Measure them with your hand to test the size of the animals' feet.

## Treasure Maps

Front map: Find the mud flats where Heron fished. Find Blackbird's cattail patch.

Back map: Which animals use the island? Which animal uses the smallest space?

## Breath of Life

We use our lungs to breathe oxygen from the air. Pond animals get oxygen in many ways. Do you remember which animal . . .

• Used both lungs *and* slimy skin to breathe?
• Breathed through its tail and jetted away?
• Breathed through a snorkel-tail?
• Carried a bubble of air under its wings?

## Mini-Monsters

You may think the "monsters" in the waterweed jungle are wild! If you magnify a drop of pond water, the mini-monsters you see are even wilder—and important first links of the food chain.

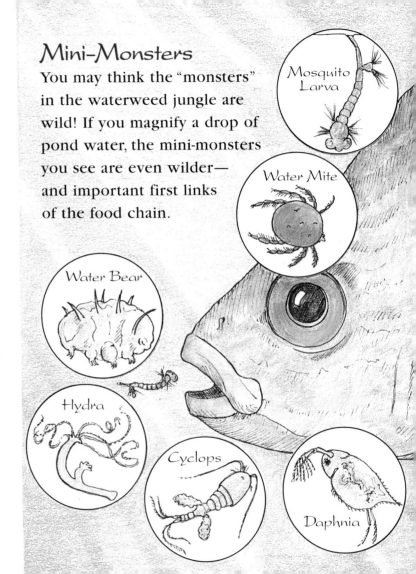

Mosquito Larva

Water Mite

Water Bear

Hydra

Cyclops

Daphnia

American history. North Carolina was the first colony to vote for independence from Great Britain. North Carolina's fight for the rights of its citizens ended in victory for all Americans.

What else comes to mind when you think of North Carolina?

- ❖ Cape Hatteras National Seashore, the longest beach on the east coast
- ❖ Dinosaur bones on display at the North Carolina Museum of Natural Sciences
- ❖ Salamanders at Great Smoky Mountains National Park, the "Salamander Capital of the World"
- ❖ The mysterious Lost Colony at Roanoke
- ❖ African Americans protesting at a lunch counter in Greensboro
- ❖ A plate of just-fried hush puppies
- ❖ Handmade furniture at High Point, the "Home Furnishings Capital of the World"
- ❖ The first succesful heavier-than-air flight at Kitty Hawk
- ❖ Reed Gold Mine, where twelve-year-old Conrad Reed's discovery of gold started the first gold rush

The Tar Heel State is special in many ways. In this book, you'll find out why. This is the story of North Carolina.

Virginia

Tennessee

Georgia

South Carolina

LITTLE TENNESSEE RIVER

©SHY01

•Asheville

Winston-Salem•

High Point•

LAKE NORMAN

• Charlotte

Greensboro

Durham

★ Raleigh

PEE DEE RIVER

ALBEMARLE SOUND

PAMLICO RIVER

PAMLICO SOUND

ATLANTIC

OCEAN

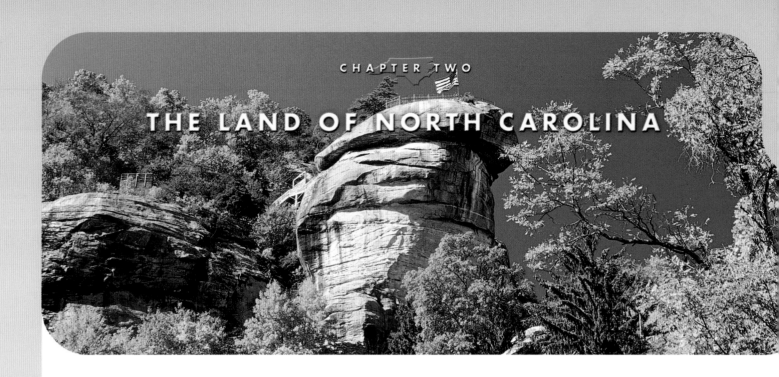

# CHAPTER TWO

# THE LAND OF NORTH CAROLINA

**Just where is North Carolina?** It is located along the southern half of the Atlantic seaboard in the eastern United States. To the west of North Carolina lies Tennessee. To the north is Virginia, and to the south are South Carolina and Georgia. These states, together with Alabama, form the region known as the Southeast.

From east to west, the land of North Carolina rises gradually. The state is divided into four land regions: the Atlantic Coastal Plain, the Outer Banks, the Piedmont, and the Mountains.

Autumn is a great time to visit Chimney Rock Park, where you can catch the view, hike the trails, and stop in at the nature center.

## THE ATLANTIC COASTAL PLAIN

The Atlantic Coastal Plain is the largest natural region in the state. It covers 25,000 square miles (64,750 square kilometers). As you travel inland about 100 miles (161 km), the area is flat and mostly swampy.

One of the swamplands, the Dismal Swamp, has eerie-looking black gum trees and cypress trees covered with moss. This swamp covers 600 square miles (1,554 sq km) of the northeastern part of the state and spreads into Virginia. Lake Drummond is one of many lakes in this area. Unusual lights, called foxfire, have been seen around this lake at night. The lights come from decaying forest wood that gives off gas. Beyond the swamp, the land becomes flat for the next hundred miles (161 km) to the west.

## THE OUTER BANKS

The Outer Banks are a string of islands that run along the coast of North Carolina. They are called barrier islands because they protect the mainland from hurri-

Dismal Swamp is a haven for birds and mammals. Many rare plants can be found there as well.

### EXTRA! EXTRA!

The Cape Hatteras Lighthouse is the tallest in the nation and is a famous symbol of North Carolina. Built in 1871, this 20-story-high lighthouse stands 208 feet (63 m) tall. Its light can be seen for over 20 miles (32 km), and it has helped sailors to navigate the sea for over 100 years. In 1999 the Atlantic Ocean threatened the lighthouse, as the tide came in closer and closer. The entire lighthouse was moved back 2900 feet (884 m) in June 1999. Today it is open to the public and you can climb all the way to the top.

The Outer Banks stick out from the coast in the shape of a foot.

canes. Like one long foot, the coastline stretches 300 miles (483 km) from Virginia to South Carolina.

The "heel" of the foot kicks out into the ocean at three points—Cape Hatteras, Cape Lookout, and Cape Fear. Many hurricanes and other fierce storms have struck Cape Hatteras. Hundreds of ships have sunk in the surrounding waters. This explains how Cape Hatteras got its nickname—the "Graveyard of the Atlantic."

## THE PIEDMONT

The central part of the state is called the Piedmont, or the foothills of North Carolina. The Piedmont rises gently upward from the coastal

### FIND OUT MORE

The environment of the Outer Banks is sandy and salty. Plants do not usually grow well in such an environment. Yet more than 300 kinds of plants exist in Nags Head Woods, a maritime forest on the Outer Banks. What makes this possible?

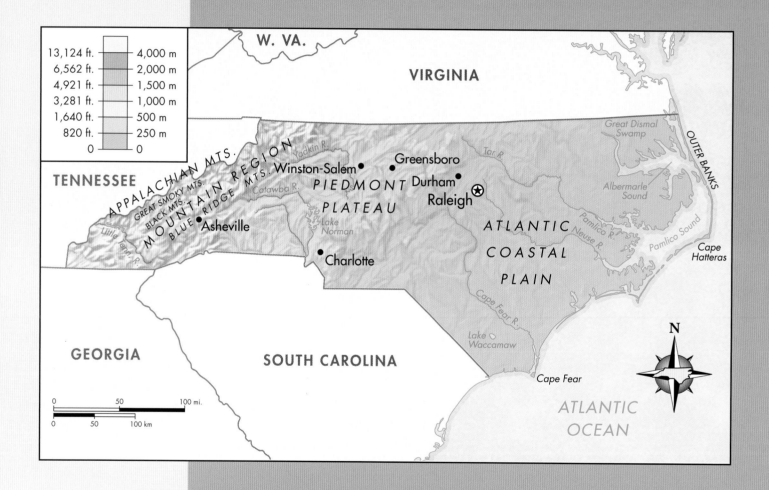

Map of North Carolina

Scale:
13,124 ft. — 4,000 m
6,562 ft. — 2,000 m
4,921 ft. — 1,500 m
3,281 ft. — 1,000 m
1,640 ft. — 500 m
820 ft. — 250 m
0 — 0

W. VA.

VIRGINIA

TENNESSEE

*APPALACHIAN MTS.*

*GREAT SMOKY MTS.*
*BLACK MTS.*
*MOUNTAIN REGION*
*BLUE RIDGE MTS.*

*Little Tenn. R.*

Asheville

*Catawba R.*

*Yadkin R.*

Winston-Salem

*PIEDMONT PLATEAU*

Greensboro

Durham

Raleigh ✪

*Lake Norman*

Charlotte

*Tar R.*

Great Dismal Swamp

OUTER BANKS

*Albermarle Sound*

*Pamlico R.*

*ATLANTIC COASTAL PLAIN*

*Neuse R.*

Pamlico Sound

Cape Hatteras

*Cape Fear R.*

*Lake Waccamaw*

Cape Fear

GEORGIA

SOUTH CAROLINA

ATLANTIC OCEAN

N

0     50     100 mi.
0     50     100 km

10

plain. An imaginary border known as the fall line divides the two regions. The land is higher to the west of the fall line, causing many waterfalls.

More people live in the Piedmont than anywhere else in the state. That's because most of North Carolina's major cities are located here, including Raleigh and Charlotte. Much of the state's manufacturing takes place in the Piedmont.

## THE MOUNTAINS

The mountains of western North Carolina begin where the Piedmont ends. These mountains are the southern part of the Appalachian Mountains that run from Pennsylvania to Georgia. North Carolina has two important mountain chains—the Blue Ridge Mountains and the Great Smoky Mountains. These are connected by other mountain ranges, including the Black Mountains. The dark evergreen forests across the peaks give the Black Mountains their name. They are the highest mountains east of the Mississippi River.

The Appalachian Trail follows the crest of Roan Mountain in North Carolina. Many people think that Roan Mountain is the most beautiful part of the Trail. The Trail is part of a path that is almost as long as the

Many people live in scenic, rural communities in the Piedmont region of North Carolina.

## FIND OUT MORE

Mount Mitchell was named after Dr. Elisha Mitchell, a professor of science at the University of North Carolina. In 1835 he discovered that this mountain was higher than Grandfather Mountain, which was thought to be the highest mountain in the region. Grandfather Mountain is 5,964 feet (1,818 m) high at its highest point, Calloway Peak. Mount Mitchell is 6,684 feet (2,037 m) high, the highest point in eastern America. How much higher is Mount Mitchell than Grandfather Mountain?

The Blue Ridge Parkway is 469 miles (755 km) of road that winds its way through the Appalachian region in North Carolina and Virginia.

Roan Mountain is one of the most beautiful mountains in the southern Appalachians. Roan Mountain State Park has eight hiking trails covering 17 miles (27 km).

United States is wide. It stretches 2,100 miles (3,380 km) from Georgia to Maine. Roan Mountain gets its name from the rhododendrons that bloom there in late spring.

## LAKES AND RIVERS

North Carolina has many lakes. Some of these lakes have been formed by dams that hold back river water. Companies like the Tennessee Valley Authority create lakes for the purpose of providing water power for electricity. The lakes also help control flooding.

In the coastal plain east of the fall line, there are natural lakes. Mattamuskeet is the state's largest natural lake. It is 15 miles (24 km) long and 6 miles (10 km) wide. Other lakes are in shallow, sunken areas known as the Carolina Bays. Some people believe that a meteor fell thousands of years ago from outer space and landed on the earth so hard that it broke into pieces and created these holes. Over time, these holes filled with water and formed lakes.

The oval shape of a Carolina Bay can be seen perfectly from the air. Carolina Bays are believed to be at least 30,000 to 100,000 years old!

Many rivers start in the mountains. In the coastal plain, the rivers slow down. The Roanoke, Neuse, Tar-Pamlico, and Cape Fear Rivers are the major rivers of the state. The Roanoke River is the

longest. It flows into Albemarle Sound in the northeastern part of the state. The Neuse and Tar Rivers in central North Carolina and Cape Fear River and South River all flow into the Atlantic Ocean. Cape Fear River is the only one that empties directly into the ocean. The Hiwasee, Little Tennessee, and Watauga Rivers flow westward from the mountains.

The Blue Ridge Mountain chain receives more than 40 inches (102 cm) of rain a year. Rainwater fills the creeks, which run into rivers, picking up speed as they flow down slopes. They roar over waterfalls, turning into whitewater rapids. Whitewater Falls is one of the largest waterfalls in the United States. It's about as tall as the Empire State Building in New York City.

Most of the lakes in western North Carolina were built by human hands. The largest is Lake Norman on the Catawba River in the west central part of the state. Other lakes include High Rock Lake on the Yadkin River, Roanoke Rapids Lake on the Roanoke River, and Roxboro Lake on the northern border of Virginia.

Between the Atlantic Ocean and the eastern border of North Carolina's mainland lie Currituck Sound, Albemarle Sound, and Pamlico Sound. Farther south are Raleigh Bay and Onslow Bay. Cape Fear is located near the southernmost end of the state.

## PLANTS AND ANIMALS

If you travel from the Outer Banks to the mountains, you'll find a whole range of plant life. The dunes of the Outer Banks are full of low shrubs such as sea oats. Trees can't survive the high ocean winds.

The wetlands lie to the west of the Outer Banks. Here you'll find salt marshes and freshwater marshes with grasses and cattails. Bald cypress trees that are 2,000 years old are in the swamps.

In the Sandhills located to the southwest of Raleigh, the soil is too sandy for plants to grow. In fact, the Sandhills were once beaches. The grass is wiry, and any flowers that grow here don't need much rain.

You'll find many forests throughout the state. The great Nantahala National Forest in the southwest has many waterfalls and whitewater rapids. Buxton Woods is the largest maritime forest in the Outer Banks.

There is less wildlife in North Carolina than there used to be because of logging and building. Still, the state has about 850 species of vertebrates, or animals and birds with a backbone, living there. Some of these animals and birds live in the Outer Banks year-round. Ducks, geese, and tundra swans come during the winter months. Herons and egrets spend the summer months here. You might also see peregrine falcons and bald eagles. Alligators live in the

Spotted salamanders are, in fact, hard to spot! They spend most of the year beneath forest litter or under the ground, and rarely come out during the day.

swamps while beavers and muskrats build their homes in the rivers. On land are rabbits, deer, squirrels, and chipmunks. Black bears and red wolves are also found in wildlife refuges like the Great Dismal Swamp.

If you head west into the Appalachian Mountains you'll be in the "Salamander Capital of the World." Salamanders thrive in moist soil, which makes the southeastern United States an ideal home. The Great Smoky Mountains National Park is crawling with salamanders. But you won't see them very often because they like to hide in rotting tree stumps, burrowed in the ground or under rocks, leaves, or logs.

Lake Waccamaw has many species of fish and mollusks. The Waccamaw silverside is only found in this lake. Jordan Lake in central North Carolina just west of Raleigh is also well known, but not for its fish— rare bald eagles nest in the upper regions.

## CLIMATE

North Carolina weather can go to extremes. On some summer days, temperatures can top 100°Fahrenheit (37.8°Celsius) while winter temperatures may drop below zero (−18°C). Temperatures are naturally higher on the coast. The Gulf Stream warms areas south of Wilmington. But if you travel through the Piedmont to the mountains you'll feel the cool air. Some of the state's highest points can be as cold as southern Canada, more than 3,000 miles (4,827 km) away.

## FIND OUT MORE

In the 1920s, European wild boars were brought to a private game preserve near the Great Smoky Mountains National Park. It wasn't long before the animals escaped and wandered into the park. How do you think they affected the balance of life in the park?

Overall, North Carolina has a mild climate, thanks to the Gulf Stream and the Blue Ridge Mountains. The Gulf Stream keeps the coastal areas mild while the mountains shield the region to the east from the cold weather of the north and northwest. The annual mean temperature in January is 40°F (4°C). In July, the annual mean temperature is 76°F (24°C).

North Carolina receives 40 to 80 inches (102 to 203 cm) of precipitation each year. The town of Cashiers gets the most rain—about 80 inches (203 cm) a year. It's the wettest place in the eastern United States! Scientists say that a tropical storm or hurricane strikes North Carolina once every four years. In September 1999, Hurricane Floyd hit the North Carolina coast with high winds and flooding.

Fierce hurricanes sometimes strike the Outer Banks, destroying many homes.

17

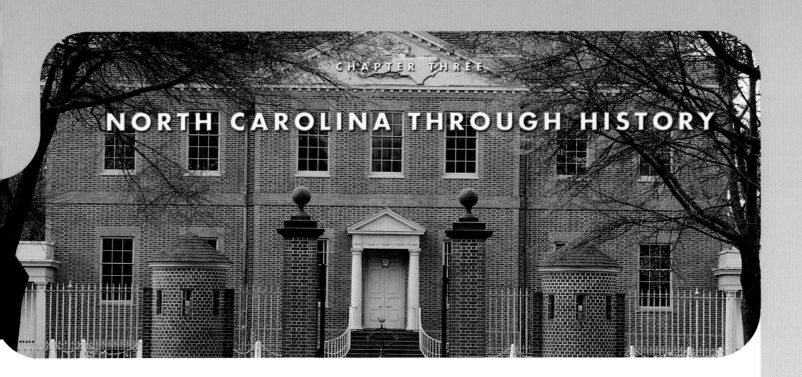

# CHAPTER THREE

# NORTH CAROLINA THROUGH HISTORY

Tryon Palace, built in 1767, was named after William Tryon, a royal governor in 1765. Today you can take a tour of the palace and its gardens.

**T**he story of North Carolina began thousands of years ago. At that time, Paleo Indians made their way across a land bridge from Asia to North America. They traveled southward and eastward hunting for buffalo and small game.

Scientists say that the first hunters reached North Carolina 11,000 years ago as the last Ice Age came to an end. The hunters settled in villages near rivers or streams. There was fresh water to drink and plenty of fish to eat. The hunters built shelters called wigwams by bending young trees and covering the trees with bark and hides. They cleared fields and planted squash, corn, and other vegetables.

Over time, Native American tribes developed and spread throughout the territory. Among these tribes were the Tuscarora, the Catawba, and the Cherokee. The Tuscaroras built their villages along the Roanoke, Pamlico, and Neuse Rivers. The English described the tribe as hostile and warlike. The Tuscaroras lived on the coastal plain until 1713, when they moved to join relatives in New York state.

The Catawba tribe settled in the Piedmont. They did not move from place to place but settled down to farm the land. Their houses were made of bark with roofs of cattails. They lived peacefully with the new settlers.

The Cherokees, the largest tribe, lived in the mountains. At first, the Cherokees lived in huts, then log hogans, wooden houses covered with hardened clay. Like the Catawba, the Cherokee tribe did not wander but settled in communities. The taller, stronger Cherokees traveled a long way to hunt for wild game, but they always came home.

The earliest Cherokee lived in what is now the western part of the state. Today, a small number of Cherokee still live in the mountains of North Carolina.

### THE EUROPEANS ARRIVE

It is likely that a man named Giovanni da Verrazzano was the first European explorer to set sight on what is now North Carolina. King Francis I of France sent out an expedition to explore across the Atlantic, and he chose Verrazzano as its leader. Verrazzano set sail with four ships and reached the coast with just one ship left in 1524. He ran into trouble on the sand banks and could not find a place to anchor his ship. So he sailed on to explore the area between Cape Fear and Kitty Hawk. Spain

This painting shows Raleigh onboard his ship during one of his voyages of discovery.

sent explorers to North Carolina a few years after France, but neither the French nor the Spanish tried to colonize the area.

In 1584, Queen Elizabeth of England appointed Sir Walter Raleigh to arrange an expedition. The explorers reached Cape Hatteras that summer and claimed the land for England. They stayed on Roanoke Island and traveled up and down the coast. They wrote reports. They drew pictures. They brought two natives, Manteo and Wanchese, back to England. Coming from the strange New World, the natives drew much attention. News of the discoveries—the crops, the fish, and the wildlife—spread throughout England. Plans to colonize the area of North Carolina grew quickly. Rich men hoping for trade offered money and supplies to Raleigh. Between 1584 and 1585, the territory was named Virginia for Queen Elizabeth, the Virgin Queen.

The same year, another fleet of ships set sail for North Carolina under Sir Richard Grenville. Most of the 107 colonists were soldiers. A few of them were merchants and "gentlemen." An artist, John White, was with them along with Raleigh's friend, a scientist, Thomas Hariot. They made maps of the area. White drew pictures of the natives as well as the plants and other living things. Even today, White's watercolor drawings are one of the most valuable sources of information about these early voyages.

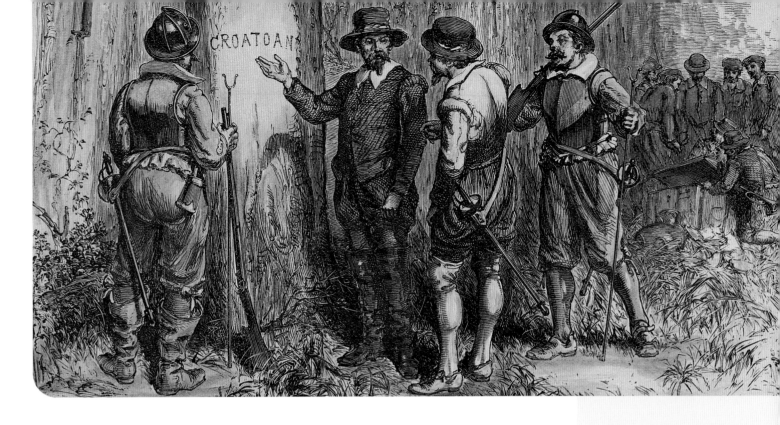

The colonists built a fort and some small houses at the northern end of Roanoke Island. When supplies ran out, Grenville, along with White and Hariot, returned to England for more. When White made his next journey back to Roanoke Island he was appointed governor. He sailed with a group of 113 settlers, including seventeen women and eleven children. When they finally arrived on the island years later, the original colony had mysteriously disappeared—only skeletons were found. The only clue was the word CROATOAN carved on a tree. To this day, no one knows what happened to the colonists.

Two children were born on Roanoke in 1587, including White's granddaughter, Virginia Dare. Virginia was the first child born of English parents in the new world. She, too, disappeared along with the rest of the colonists on Roanoke.

The only clue left on Roanoke Island was the word CROATOAN carved into a tree.

In 1629, King Charles I of England gave Sir Robert Heath a charter to the entire southern part of Britain's claim to America. Heath was the king's legal adviser and named the new territory *New Carolana* after King Charles. This area included both North Carolina and South Carolina.

In 1663, King Charles II took the Carolina charter away from Heath and gave it to eight of his friends, who were called Lords Proprietors. These ruling landowners did not want to leave their homes in England, so they ruled the colony from England by appointing governors to act on their behalf.

The colonists, however, did not want to be governed by England. In Albemarle, the colonists arrested their governor in 1677 and elected John Culpeper, a land surveyor, to govern the colony. For two years Culpeper acted as governor until he was finally removed by the English landowners.

By 1680, 5,000 new settlers had arrived. They were poor farmers who moved into areas occupied by Native American tribes. In 1706 the first permanent town of Bath was established. Five years later, the Tuscarora tribe rose up against the settlers and killed many of them. The Tuscarora War of 1711 raged on for eighteen months. The Tuscaroras burned the settlers' homes, destroyed their crops, and drove off or

## WHAT'S IN A NAME?

Many names of places in North Carolina have interesting origins.

| Name | Comes from or means |
| --- | --- |
| Carolina | Carolus is Latin for "Charles" |
| Kitty Hawk | Poteskeet word meaning "Chickahauk" |
| Charlotte | Queen Charlotte, wife of Britain's King George III |
| Cape Hatteras | Hatteras Native Americans |
| Raleigh | Sir Walter Raleigh, English explorer |
| Mount Mitchell | Dr. Elisha Mitchell, science professor |
| Roanoke River | Roanoke Native Americans |
| Catawba River | Catawba Native Americans |
| Tar River | tar, forest product |

killed livestock. In the end, many Tuscaroras were captured, killed, or sold into slavery as a result of the war.

Throughout the early 1700s, pirates also raided the coastal towns. One of the most famous pirates was Edward Teach, known as Blackbeard. He was killed in a battle near Ocracoke Island in 1718. Some believe that Blackbeard's stolen treasure is still buried there.

To keep the growing colony successful, indentured servants were hired for a period of four to seven years to work the farms. Some servants were paid for their work. As the colony grew, more and more servants were needed. Plantation owners, people who owned large pieces of land, began importing people from Africa to work as slaves. Slaves were not paid for their work, and they were "owned" by their master, the landowner. Enslaved Africans worked on plantations for their entire lives.

In 1729 the Lords Proprietors sold their interests in the colony to King George II. It then became a royal colony ruled by the king's governor. Settlers from Britain and other colonies filled the territory. Many came from Pennsylvania, Virginia, and South Carolina. North Carolina's population grew rapidly. By 1750, North Carolina had 75,000 people. By 1775, the number of people living there reached 350,000.

Blackbeard was the most feared pirate on the high seas. He was eventually killed in battle with the Royal Navy.

## THE PATH TO FREEDOM

Throughout the colonization of America, there were many wars. The British and the French fought over the same land. The French and the Spanish fought over the southern part of North Carolina. The settlers

Parts of the French and Indian War were fought in North Carolina. Fort Dobbs was the scene of an important victory for the British.

fought with Native Americans. Some Native Americans sided with the British; others, with the French. In 1754 war broke out between the British and the French, although it wasn't officially declared until 1756. Britain won the French and Indian War (1754–1763) and forced France to give up its claims in North America.

The war cost Britain a lot of money. To help pay for it, Britain placed heavy taxes on English products sold in the colonies, charging more for these goods. Money was scarce, however, and in 1771 a group of farmers in North Carolina formed a group called The Regulators. To protest colonial taxation, they started riots and fired at British troops. Governor Tryon sent more than 1,000 British soldiers to put down the rebellion at the Battle of Alamance Creek. The Regulators were defeated.

North Carolina wasn't the only colony against taxes. Other colonies spoke out, and eventually the taxes were removed from all products except tea. Even the tea tax, however, wasn't acceptable, and protests such as the Boston Tea Party in Massachusetts and the Edenton Tea Party in North Carolina took place. The Edenton Tea Party was organized by a group of North Carolina women who declared that they would drink no more tea, declaring a boycott. This was the first time that American women became involved in politics. Tea was eventually boycotted throughout the colonies.

In the town of Edenton, this teapot is mounted on a Revolutionary cannon to serve as a reminder of the Edenton Tea Party.

Resistance to British rule was growing stronger. On May 31, 1775, a group of citizens from Mecklenburg, North Carolina, drew up a document called the Mecklenburg Resolves, declaring freedom from Britain. North Carolina was the first colony to say that it was ready to fight for independence.

North Carolina's official declaration of freedom inspired the other colonies. The desire for freedom was so great that the American Revolutionary War (1775–1783) broke out between Britain and the American colonies. Colonists in North Carolina took opposing sides. The Tories, or Loyalists, wanted British rule. The Whigs, or Patriots, wanted independence. The first battle of the war fought in North Carolina took place on February 2, 1776, at Moore's Creek Bridge.

Meanwhile, representatives from each state had formed a group called the Continental Congress. This group met twice, first in 1774 and again in 1775, when they established the Continental Army headed by George Washington. In 1776 they officially declared independence from Britain by creating a document called the Declaration of Independence. This document stated the reasons why the colonies should be independent of Britain. Two delegates from North Carolina, Joseph Hewes and John Penn, signed the Declaration of Independence on behalf of the state.

A major turning point of the war was the Battle of Guilford Courthouse in Greensboro. Britain won this battle, but their army was terribly weakened—they lost one out of every four soldiers. Seven months later, General Cornwallis, leader of the British troops, surrendered his army at Yorktown, Virginia. The war ended in October 1781, and a peace treaty was signed in 1783.

Once the war was over, plans to create a central government began. Out of these plans was formed the United States Constitution, which established the first system of government. Several states, including North Carolina, feared that the Constitution gave too much power to the federal government. They refused to approve the Federal Constitution without amendments, or changes,

## FAMOUS FIRSTS

- North Carolina was the first colony to declare independence from Great Britain
- The first gold rush in the United States started at Reed Gold Mine in 1803
- The University of North Carolina was the first state university in the United States
- The United States opened the first branch of the mint in Charlotte in 1837
- Orville and Wilbur Wright flew the first powered airplane at Kitty Hawk in 1903
- The first protest against segregation took place in Greensboro

General Cornwallis' surrender to General Washington at Yorktown ended the American Revolution.

called the Bill of Rights. When the changes were added, North Carolina signed the Constitution in 1789. North Carolina was the twelfth colony to enter the Union.

## THE BEGINNING OF INDEPENDENCE

In the early 1800s, North Carolina had many small farms and a few large plantations. Tobacco and cotton were major crops. The invention of the cotton gin in 1793 increased production of cotton. However, growing the same two crops year after year drained the soil's nutrients. Heavy rains washed away the topsoil, and the damaged soil produced bad crops for many years. Farmers who owned small farms moved out of the state. One out of three people left North Carolina.

In 1835, North Carolina changed its state constitution to allow most male white landowners to vote. After this change, rich plantation owners no longer controlled government. The state legislature voted to develop land for farming in the western part of the state. Another change in the constitution took away the voting rights of free African Americans. This change made a clear division between the two groups.

There was no new economic growth in North Carolina during the first thirty years of the nineteenth century. The government did nothing to help the state grow. As a matter of fact, it seemed as if the state had fallen asleep, like Washington Irving's famous story character, Rip Van Winkle. North Carolina became known as the "Rip Van Winkle State."

By the 1850s the issue of how much power the Union should have over the states came up in North Carolina, along with many other southern states. The northern states opposed slavery. Many people in the southern states wanted to keep slavery. North Carolina was a slave state because it was south of the Mason-Dixon line at the Pennsylvania-Maryland boundary. The Union was split in two.

By 1860 at least 300,000 enslaved African Americans lived in North Carolina. That amounted to one out of three people in the state. However, North Carolina did not have as many slaves as other southern states. Most white people in North Carolina did not own slaves, but they also didn't question slavery as an institution. Slavery was considered essential to the state's agriculture.

North Carolina, however, was one of the original thirteen colonies and, at first, did not want to leave the Union. The turning point came in 1861, when President Abraham Lincoln wanted to put an end to slavery in the South. Many southern states seceded, or separated, from the Union to form the Confederate States of America. President Lincoln

Most of the hard work on southern plantations was done by enslaved African Americans.

Civil War soldiers proudly sent home photographs of themselves to record their participation in the war.

asked North Carolina for troops to fight the Confederacy. The North Carolina legislature refused and instead voted to secede from the Union. North Carolina was the last southern state to do so.

At least 125,000 North Carolinians fought in the Confederate Army. One out of every four Southerners killed in the Civil War (1861–1865) was from North Carolina. The state lost nearly 20,000 men in the war, more than any other southern state. Ten important Civil War battles were fought in North Carolina. The bloodiest was at Bentonville, in 1865. This is where North Carolina surrendered its army to the Unionists.

After the war, North Carolina lay in ruins. Towns had been burned and farmland wasted. Between 1867 and 1878, federal troops controlled

In Berne, North Carolina, people waited in long lines to get clothing during the time of Reconstruction.

North Carolina. This was a time of rebuilding America, called the Reconstruction Era. North Carolina entered the Union again in 1868.

In 1863, Abraham Lincoln had issued the Emancipation Proclamation which declared freedom for all slaves in the South. Former slaves, without money and without homes, wandered from place to place. They began to participate in a free society. For the first time, African Americans could vote. Some even entered politics by joining the Republican Party of Abraham Lincoln.

Members of the Ku Klux Klan burned crosses as a way of terrorizing African Americans.

## AFTER THE WAR

In 1868 there was much disagreement about the newly won rights of African Americans. A group of whites called the Ku Klux Klan terrorized African Americans throughout the entire south. "Jim Crow" laws were created that called for segregation, or separation, of white people from African Americans. African-American children were not allowed to attend school with white children. There were separate waiting rooms at bus and train stations. African Americans could not be buried in ground set aside for the burial of white people.

Throughout the Reconstruction Era, North Carolina struggled with a bad economy. Fewer crops were being produced and sold. Many of the

During segregation, a young African-American child is forced to drink out of a water fountain marked "colored."

slaves who had worked in tobacco and cotton fields left the plantations and headed north to find better jobs. Other poor African Americans and poor whites rented land from the planters. But the rents were high, forcing farmers to pay by sharing crops with their landowners. This was called sharecropping.

Until the late 1800s, North Carolina was still a farming state with tobacco and cotton as its main crops. In 1880 three times more cotton was produced than in 1860. To process the cotton, textile mills were started throughout the Piedmont. This industrial development was known as the Cotton Mill Campaign. By the early 1900s, North Carolina's textile mills were the state's chief employer. Towns developed around the mills, and workers lived in houses that were supplied by their employers. Farming was no longer the main industry. Farmers were getting poorer because crop prices were too low and farm expenses were high.

About the same time, a major event took place in North Carolina. Two brothers, Orville and Wilbur Wright, came from Ohio to the North Carolina coast to fly their new invention—a glider with a small engine. In 1903 the Wright brothers flew the first powered flying machine at Kitty Hawk for twelve seconds. This would later provide a new way to travel.

In 1917 the United States entered World War I (1914–1918). More than 86,000 soldiers from North Carolina fought in the war. Army training camps were established around the state. Camp Greene at Charlotte was the largest. Camp Polk was at Raleigh. Both camps were closed after the war. Fort Bragg, near Fayetteville, remained open and would become the largest training center of its kind in the United States.

North Carolinians were hit hard during the Great Depression (1929–1939), a major crisis throughout the United States that caused the value of goods to drop to almost nothing. Poverty touched everywhere across the United States. Farmers lost their farms because they

The Wright Brothers chose Kitty Hawk for their first flight because of its high winds, which averaged 13 miles per hour.

## WHO'S WHO IN NORTH CAROLINA?

**Josephus Daniels (1862–1948)** was the publisher of a major North Carolina newspaper, the *News & Observer*. He also served as Secretary of the Navy (1913–1921) under President Woodrow Wilson.

33

could not sell their crops. Other people lost their homes and businesses. Eighteen banks in North Carolina were closed. It wasn't until the beginning of World War II (1939–1945) that the country finally began to recover. The United States entered the war in 1941.

Manufactured goods were needed during the war. More jobs were created and people started spending money again. Demand rose again for North Carolina's products. By the 1950s, manufacturing was growing faster in North Carolina than in other states. This continued through the 1970s and the early 1980s. But the country sank into a slump in the 1990s, and North Carolina opened its doors to new, high-tech industries. Soon, these types of industries became even more important than manufacturing in North Carolina.

## GROWTH AND CHANGE

Social change was about to happen nationwide. In 1954 the United States Supreme Court ruled that segregating black students from white students in school was against the United States Constitution. North Carolina fought the ruling by agreeing to pay private school tuition for any child "assigned to a public school attended by a child of another race." North Carolina also allowed school districts to close their schools rather than let African Americans attend school with white children. These laws were later overturned.

African Americans began protesting segregation in public places. In 1960, four African-American students sat down at a lunch counter for

After four African-American students were refused service at this Woolworth's lunch counter, many other students filled the chairs for days after, shutting down business.

whites only in an F. W. Woolworth's store in Greensboro. They refused to leave until they were served, coming back day after day. The action of these students set off a similar chain of protests across the South. Three years later, Congress passed the Civil Rights Act of 1964. This act desegregated all public places by law. By the 1970s whites and African Americans were attending public school together in North Carolina.

## EXTRA! EXTRA!

Today, the Greensboro Woolworth's is closed. In 1993, two of the original four protestors bought the store, and had plans to reopen it as "The International Civil Rights Center and Museum." There was some controversy over the project and it has since come to a standstill. A section of the Woolworth's counter and newsclips are now on display at the National Museum of American History in Washington, D.C.

Throughout the 1960s and 1970s, the state began spending more money on public schools. Interest in books, art, and music grew.

In 1985 North Carolina created the Basic Education Program by developing better study programs for students. Now there are more than 1,500 elementary schools and 300 secondary schools in the state. North Carolina also has many private schools, some of which are run by churches. The Carolina Agency for Jewish Education offers educational programs to both Jewish and non-Jewish North Carolinians.

Duke University, in Durham, was founded in 1924.

Many colleges and universities are located throughout the state. The University of North Carolina has sixteen schools in various cities, including Chapel Hill and Charlotte. Duke University in Durham is one of the best in the United States. Salem College was the first privately run college in North Carolina and one of the first women's colleges in the United States. The state also has 58 community colleges.

But while North Carolina was working to improve the state, many people moved out. They went to northern cities to look for better-paying jobs. To bring business back, North Carolina lowered taxes. In 1961 the state created a 5,000-acre (2,000-hectare) research park located in the middle of Chapel Hill, Durham, and Raleigh. (If you look on a map you'll see that these three cities can be connected with a triangle.) Through the years, Research Triangle Park grew to 7,000 acres (2,832 hectares). As a result, people started returning to the state by the 1980s. Today, the Park has 140 organizations employing 44,000 people. North Carolina is a booming state.

# CHAPTER FOUR

# GOVERNING NORTH CAROLINA

The historic House chamber is at the state capitol in Raleigh.

**N**orth Carolinians have always been independent. North Carolina was one of the original thirteen colonies, and it was the first colony to vote for independence from Great Britain. North Carolinians defined the basic principles by which it would govern its people in a document known as the constitution, adopted in 1776. In 1868 they wrote a second constitution that was later amended, or changed, thirty times to create laws of segregation, and to take away voting power from African Americans. In 1971 North Carolina wrote a third constitution. It declared that "all elections shall be free" and that the state would not treat one group of people better than another because of race, color, or religion. This constitution is still used today.

The state government of North Carolina is similar to the federal government of the United States. Both governments have three branches—the executive, the legislative, and the judicial. Together,

This statue in Raleigh commemorates three presidents who were born in North Carolina—Andrew Jackson, Andrew Johnson, and James Polk.

these branches of government make and carry out laws that protect the welfare of all citizens.

## THE EXECUTIVE BRANCH

The executive branch enforces the state's laws. North Carolina's governor is head of the executive branch. He or she is elected for a four-year term by the people of North Carolina, and can only be elected twice.

The governor has several duties. One of the most important is planning the state's budget. The budget shows how much money the state can spend on services for its citizens. The governor can also propose laws or veto (say no to) laws that the legislature passed. The governor is also the commander-in-chief of the state's military forces and can call out the militia to protect North Carolina's citizens if necessary.

## THE LEGISLATIVE BRANCH

The legislative branch of government makes new laws. North Carolina laws may focus on building schools and other public buildings and highways. Paying for health care and reducing crime are other problems that come before the legislature. The legislature also studies the budget recommended by the governor and decides how much money the state will pay to educate, protect, and help its citizens.

## WHO'S WHO IN NORTH CAROLINA?

**Senator Jesse Helms** (1921– ) was born in Monroe. He served five terms in the U.S. Senate between 1973 and 2003. He is the first North Carolinian to receive the Golden Gavel for presiding over the Senate more than 117 hours in 1973, and more than 120 hours in 1974.

The legislative building in Raleigh includes both the Senate and House Chambers.

The capitol building in Raleigh replaced the old state house, which burned down in 1831.

The members of the legislative branch are called the General Assembly. They meet once a year at the Legislative Building in Raleigh. The General Assembly is made up of two groups—the House of Representatives and the Senate. The House of Representatives has 120 members, and the Senate has 50 members. Each member of the legislature is elected to serve for two years.

## THE JUDICIAL BRANCH

The judicial branch is the state's court system, which interprets the laws. In a dispute, the courts hear both sides of a case to decide whether or not laws have been broken. The courts also decide on the penalty.

# NORTH CAROLINA STATE GOVERNMENT

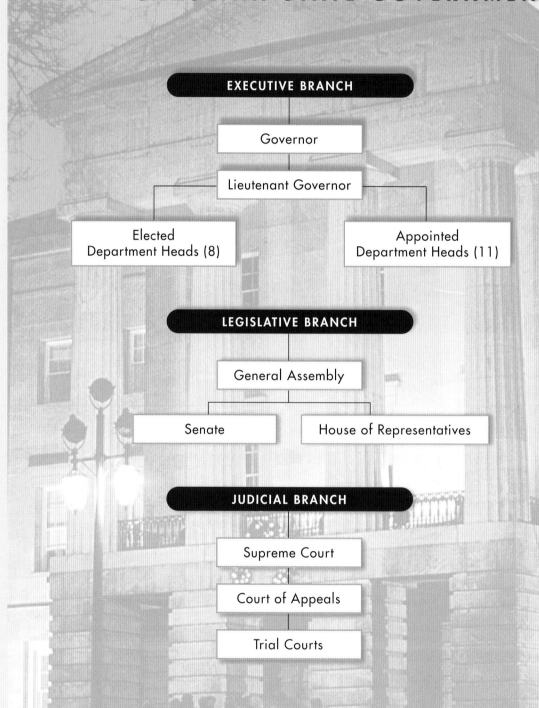

**EXECUTIVE BRANCH**

Governor

Lieutenant Governor

Elected Department Heads (8)

Appointed Department Heads (11)

**LEGISLATIVE BRANCH**

General Assembly

Senate

House of Representatives

**JUDICIAL BRANCH**

Supreme Court

Court of Appeals

Trial Courts

# NORTH CAROLINA GOVERNORS

| Name | Term | Name | Term |
|---|---|---|---|
| Richard Caswell | 1776–1780 | Z.B. Vance | 1862–1865 |
| Abner Nash | 1780–1781 | W.W. Holden (provisional governor) | 1865 |
| Thomas Burke | 1781–1782 | Jonathan Worth | 1865–1868 |
| Alexander Martin | 1782–1784 | W.W. Holden | 1868–1871 |
| Richard Caswell | 1784–1787 | T.R. Caldwell | 1871–1874 |
| Samuel Johnston | 1787–1789 | C.H. Brogden | 1874–1877 |
| Alexander Martin | 1789–1792 | Z.B. Vance | 1877–1879 |
| R.D. Spaight Sr. | 1792–1795 | T.J. Jarvis | 1879–1885 |
| Samuel Ashe | 1795–1798 | A.M. Scalees | 1885–1889 |
| W.R. Davie | 1798–1799 | D.G. Fowle | 1889–1891 |
| Benjamin Williams | 1799–1802 | Thomas M. Holt | 1891–1893 |
| James Turner | 1802–1805 | Elias Carr | 1893–1897 |
| Nathaniel Alexander | 1805–1807 | D.L. Russell | 1897–1901 |
| Benjamin Williams | 1807–1808 | Charles B. Aycock | 1901–1905 |
| David Stone | 1808–1810 | R.B. Glenn | 1905–1909 |
| Benjamin Smith | 1810–1811 | W.W. Kitchin | 1909–1913 |
| William Hawkins | 1811–1814 | Locke Craig | 1913–1917 |
| William Miller | 1814–1817 | Thomas W. Bickett | 1917–1921 |
| John Branch | 1817–1820 | Cameron Morrison | 1921–1925 |
| Jesse Franklin | 1820–1821 | Angus Wilton McLean | 1925–1929 |
| Gabriel Holmes | 1821–1824 | O. Max Gardner | 1929–1933 |
| H.G. Burton | 1824–1827 | J.C.B. Ehringhaus | 1933–1937 |
| James Iredell Jr. | 1827–1828 | Clyde R. Hoey | 1937–1941 |
| John Owen | 1828–1830 | J. Melville Broughton | 1941–1945 |
| Montfort Stokes | 1830–1832 | R. Gregg Cherry | 1945–1949 |
| D.L. Swain | 1832–1835 | W. Kerr Scott | 1949–1953 |
| R.D. Spaight Jr. | 1835–1836 | William B. Umstead | 1953–1954 |
| E.B. Dudley | 1836–1841 | Luther H. Hodges | 1954–1961 |
| J.M. Morehead | 1841–1845 | Terry Sanford | 1961–1965 |
| W.A. Graham | 1845–1849 | Daniel K. Moore | 1965–1969 |
| Charles Manly | 1849–1851 | Robert W. Scott | 1969–1973 |
| D.S. Reid | 1851–1854 | James E. Holshouser Jr. | 1973–1977 |
| Warren Winslow | 1854–1855 | James B. Hunt Jr. | 1977–1985 |
| Thomas Bragg | 1855–1859 | James G. Martin | 1985–1993 |
| John W. Ellis | 1859–1861 | James B. Hunt Jr. | 1993–2001 |
| Henry T. Clark | 1861–1862 | Michael F. Easley | 2001–2008 |

Raleigh is a booming city with many new people and businesses moving in each year.

District courts hear civil cases that involve less than $10,000 and don't involve a crime. Civil cases are disputes that may involve unlawful activities, such as a dispute between a group of citizens and a city about the use of a public building. District courts also handle cases involving young people.

At the next level, the Court of Appeals reviews cases ruled on by the lower courts and determines whether or not the correct decision was made. The Court of Appeals may overturn (reverse) or uphold the lower court's decision. There are twelve judges in the Court of Appeals.

If the court upholds the lower ruling, the case may be appealed to the state Supreme Court, the state's highest court. A chief justice and six justices preside over the state Supreme Court. The decision of this court is final.

All North Carolina judges are elected. District judges serve a term of four years. Other justices and judges serve eight years.

## TAKE A TOUR OF RALEIGH, THE STATE CAPITAL

Raleigh is known as the "City of Oaks" because it has many trees and parks. It is one of the fastest growing cities in the United States—more than 280,000 people live here! Many scientists and businesspeople have come from all over the world to work at nearby Research Triangle Park.

Raleigh is laid out in a grid pattern with the capitol building in the center. The capitol was built in 1840. Today it is a national historic

Raleigh is a mix of old and new. The Oakwood Historic District has many old homes dating back to the nineteenth century.

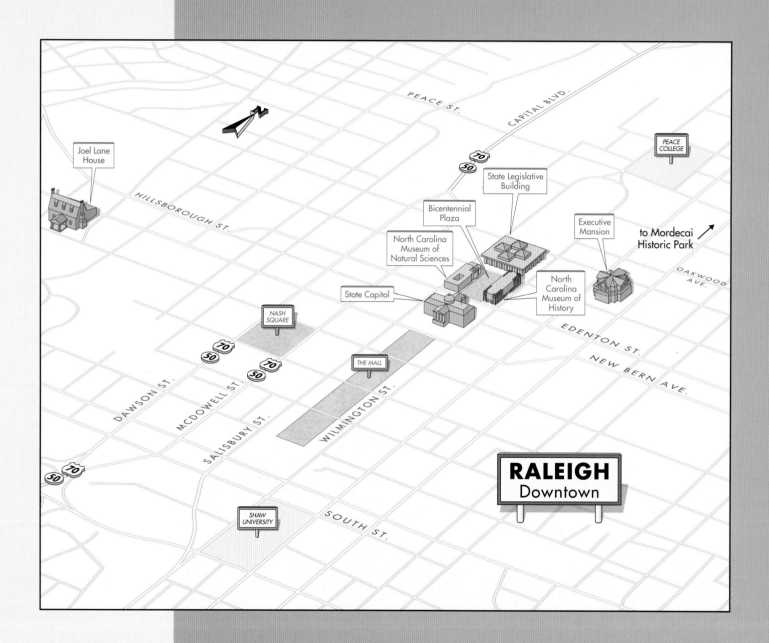

Joel Lane
House

PEACE ST.

CAPITAL BLVD.

PEACE
COLLEGE

70
50

State Legislative
Building

Bicentennial
Plaza

HILLSBOROUGH ST.

Executive
Mansion

to Mordecai
Historic Park

North Carolina
Museum of
Natural Sciences

OAKWOOD
AVE.

North
Carolina
Museum of
History

State Capitol

NASH
SQUARE

70
50

EDENTON ST.

70
50

NEW BERN AVE.

THE MALL

DAWSON ST.

MCDOWELL ST.

SALISBURY ST.

WILMINGTON ST.

**RALEIGH**
Downtown

70
50

SHAW
UNIVERSITY

SOUTH ST.

landmark. The building is shaped like a cross with a copper dome rising ten stories above it. Under the dome is a life-size statue of George Washington dressed like a Roman general. At one time, all government offices were located in the capitol, but today only the executive offices, including the governor's office, are here.

If you walk one block north of the capitol you'll find the State Legislative Building. When the General Assembly is in session, you can watch lawmakers in action from the gallery upstairs.

Close by is the Oakwood Historic District. This section of the city has more than 400 private homes, all built in the 1800s. The oldest

North Carolina's Executive Mansion is listed on the National Register of Historic Places. It was built in 1891.

home in Raleigh is the Wakefield, or Joel Lane House. Built in 1760, it was named for Margaret Wake, the wife of a royal governor. Colonel Joel Lane, the "father of Raleigh," lived in the house. In 1792 he sold 1,000 acres (400 hectares) of land to the state for its capital. Today, the governor and his family live in the Executive Mansion, not far away from the Oakwood Historic District.

Andrew Johnson, the seventeenth president of the United States (1865–1869), was born in Raleigh in 1808. You can visit his birthplace on Village Street in Mordecai Historic Park.

Another stop on the tour is the African American Cultural Complex, where you'll learn about the history of African Americans. Three cottages are filled with exhibits, an outdoor stage, and nature trails. On display are African masks, inventions of African Americans (such as a saddle invented by African-American cowboys), and exhibits about well-known African-American women. Forty thousand people a year visit this museum and educational center.

You'll need plenty of time to tour the next stop— the North Carolina Museum of Natural Sciences. It is the largest natural history museum in the southeast. You'll learn all about the natural world through exhibits like Mountains to the Sea, which recreates five North Carolina habitats, complete with live animals and waterfalls. You can also see a fossilized dinosaur heart, and whale skeletons of coastal Carolina. If you prefer getting your hands dirty, check out the interactive exhibits, where you can examine objects through microscopes, listen to the ocean in a sea shell, and touch fossils, rocks, and even bird wings.

Andrew Johnson was the seventeenth United States president. He took over after Abraham Lincoln's death.

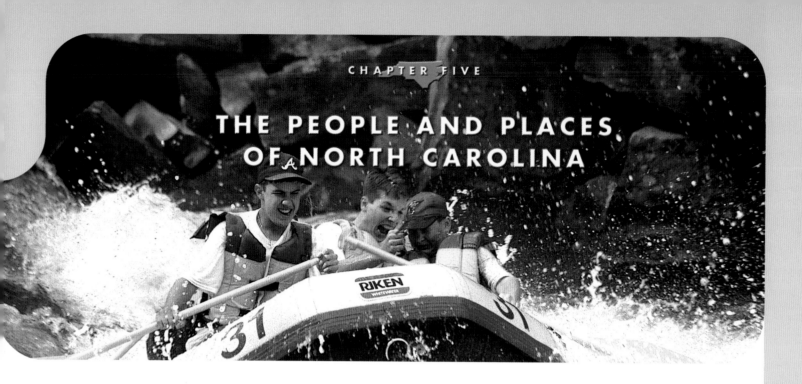

# CHAPTER FIVE

# THE PEOPLE AND PLACES OF NORTH CAROLINA

The Nantahala River is a popular place for whitewater rafting.

**N**orth Carolina ranks twenty-ninth in size compared to other states. But a lot of people live here—so many, in fact, that North Carolina is the eleventh most populated state! Many different races and ethnic backgrounds are represented by its people.

## MEET THE PEOPLE

According to the 2000 Census, more than eight million people live in the Tar Heel State. North Carolina is one of the fastest-growing states in the country. About 72 out of every 100 people are of European descent. African Americans make up the second largest group, with 22 out of every 100 people. The number of Asians and Hispanics took a big jump in the 1990s. About seven out of 100 people are either Hispanic or Native American, and almost two out of 100 people are Asian.

A diversity of races is represented in North Carolina's schools.

In the last ten years, people have been steadily spilling out of North Carolina's big cities and into the mountains and coastal areas. Nearly half of all North Carolinians live in small towns and rural areas. North Carolinians are country folks at heart. Country cooking is popular—everything from grits to fried catfish and sweet potato pie.

Many North Carolinians prefer to live in rural areas and small towns like Waynesville.

Still, some people have left farm life for city life. Charlotte is the largest city in North Carolina. The other six urban centers are in the Piedmont region and can be grouped into two geographical areas: the Triad and the Triangle. The state capital, Raleigh, along with Durham and Chapel Hill—two major university towns—form the Triangle. Research Triangle Park is in the center.

The Triad is made up of Greensboro, Winston-Salem, and High Point. Greensboro and Winston-Salem have historic importance. At the Battle of Guilford Courthouse in 1781, one out of four British soldiers was killed or wounded. This weakened the British troops and helped the Americans win the Revolutionary War. The site of the first settlement of Moravians, a religious group from Germany, is in Winston-Salem. High Point is the "Home Furnishings Capital of the World" with over 125 furniture factories.

Tours are conducted at many of North Carolina's furniture factories.

Hush puppies are a popular side dish from North Carolina. When you finish making this recipe, you'll have a lot of corny "pups!" Remember, get a grown-up to help you.

### HUSH PUPPIES

2 cups yellow cornmeal
1 cup plain flour
2 eggs
1 cup buttermilk (or substitute regular milk)
3/4 teaspoon seasoned salt
1/2 teaspoon ground pepper blend
1 teaspoon baking powder
2/3 teaspoon baking soda
1/8 cup low-fat cooking oil

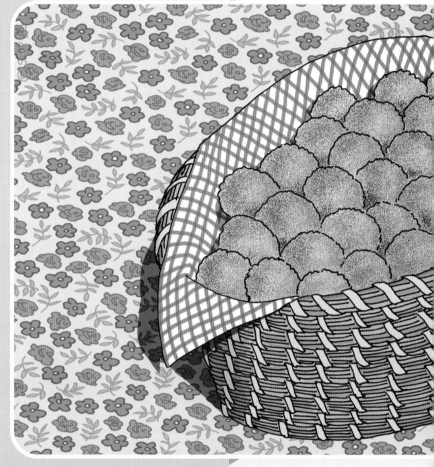

1. Fill a frying pan half full with cooking oil. Heat over medium-high heat.
2. Mix the cornmeal, flour, seasoned salt, pepper, baking powder, and baking soda in a bowl.
3. Add the eggs, oil, and buttermilk. Stir until blended.
4. Using a tablespoon, drop the batter into the frying pan.
5. Brown them on all sides. The hush puppies will float when done. Do not overcook.

## WORKING IN NORTH CAROLINA

In the early days, most North Carolinians were farmers. They lived off the crops of the land—tobacco and cotton. In 1960 North Carolina had about 212,000 farms. Now there are about 48,000 farms, but agriculture is still the state's number one industry. Almost 22 out of every 100 people work in farming. North Carolina's farmers produce more tobacco and sweet potatoes than any other state. Other farmers raise hogs and cattle. North Carolina's farmers produce crops and livestock worth about $40 billion a year.

Tobacco is still one of North Carolina's most important crops.

Many of North Carolina's service jobs are in sales, insurance, and real estate. Service workers also sell textiles, tobacco products, and furniture. Textile producers built factories in North Carolina and elsewhere in the South because wages are relatively low. One out of every three other service workers in North Carolina are doctors and nurses, lawyers, teachers, insurance salespeople, repair technicians, and government employees.

High-tech industry has created a lot of jobs in North Carolina. Thousands of scientists, engineers, and computer technicians work in the research divisions of major corporations at Research Triangle Park west of Raleigh. It is the largest research park in the United States. Many people are also employed by banks. In the 1980s, Charlotte developed into a major banking center, and today the state ranks second in the nation in the banking industry.

About one out of every three people in North Carolina work in manufacturing. As many as 900,000 people work in factories. The value of their products is nearly $60 billion a year. After North Carolina's first

Many people who live in the "triangle"—Raleigh, Chapel Hill, and Durham—are employed at Research Triangle Park.

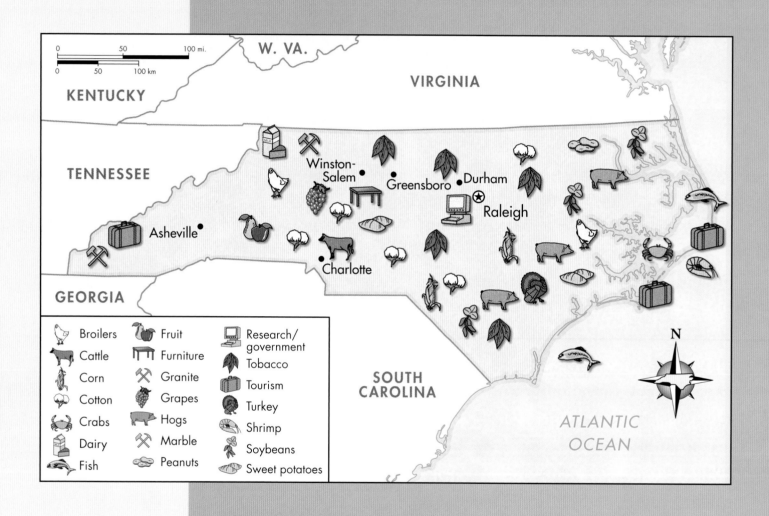

**KENTUCKY**

**W. VA.**

**VIRGINIA**

**TENNESSEE**

Winston-Salem

Greensboro

Durham

Raleigh

Asheville

Charlotte

**GEORGIA**

**SOUTH CAROLINA**

**ATLANTIC OCEAN**

N

0 50 100 mi.

0 50 100 km

Broilers
Cattle
Corn
Cotton
Crabs
Dairy
Fish

Fruit
Furniture
Granite
Grapes
Hogs
Marble
Peanuts

Research/government
Tobacco
Tourism
Turkey
Shrimp
Soybeans
Sweet potatoes

cotton mill was built in 1813, textiles became the main industry. Today, 2,100 textile plants produce sheets, towels, denim, and other items.

The fishing and seafood industry brings in about $65 million. Morehead City and Beaufort are major fishing ports in the state. Morehead City hosts a Seafood Festival every year to educate the public about seafood and its importance to the state's economy. The Festival also recognizes the many men and women who work in the fishing industry. North Carolina is careful to protect its waters from overfishing, a problem that occurred in the mid-1990s. Today, the harvesting of fish is controlled so that the people of North Carolina—and the rest of the country—will continually have fish for sale in their grocery stores.

Tourism is also a big industry in North Carolina. Every year, tourists spend about $10 billion visiting North Carolina's famous sites and recreation areas of national and state parks. The travel industry is as important as manufacturing and agriculture in North Carolina.

## TAKING A TOUR OF NORTH CAROLINA

### Eastern North Carolina and the Outer Banks

Beaches line the coast of North Carolina. The Cape Hatteras National Seashore alone stretches 72 miles (116 km). It was the first national seashore in the United States. A short ferry ride will take you to Cape Lookout National Seashore, which extends 55 miles (89 km).

There are many historic sites to visit all along the coast. The story of the Lost Colony on Roanoke Island is told through an outdoor play

The Historic Jones House, built in 1808, is in New Bern's historic district.

every night at the Fort Raleigh National Historic Site in Manteo. Fort Raleigh is where Sir Walter Raleigh tried to start an English settlement. The Wright Brothers National Memorial to the first powered airplane flight is at Kill Devil Hill. (You can't miss it because it looks like the tail of an airplane.) Fort Fisher and Fort Macon are worth seeing, too. Both forts fell to Union armies during the Civil War. Then, travel on to Ocracoke Island to see the port where Blackbeard hid to plan his attack on ships from Europe.

Several coastal towns, like Bath and New Bern, have historic districts. The buildings in these districts look the same as they did in the 1700s. St. Thomas Episcopal Church, the oldest church in the state, is located in Bath. New Bern was the colony's first capital. The largest historic district is in Wilmington. It covers 200 blocks. You can take a carriage ride to see the old homes and gardens, or cruise on the river. The battleship *North Carolina* is docked just beyond the downtown area. This ship was used in every major naval attack in the Pacific Ocean during World War II.

## Central North Carolina

Most of North Carolina's cities are in the Piedmont, or central North Carolina. More than 500,000 people live in Charlotte, the largest city in the state. As a matter of fact, it was the second fastest-growing city of its size in the last ten years. At 174.3 square miles (451 sq km), Charlotte is a big presence in the state. Even the top of the 60-story Bank of America Corporate Center looks like a crown.

### FIND OUT MORE

Battleship *North Carolina* used signal flags out at sea during World War II. Signal flags were used to communicate between two ships. There are 26 square flags that depict the letters of the alphabet, and each flag has a certain meaning. For example, a white flag with a red diamond stands for "F" or "foxtrot," which means that a ship is disabled. Find out what the other 25 flags look like. Use colored pencils to draw the signal flags that spell your first name.

Lowe's Motor Speedway in Charlotte is used for stock car racing.

Charlotte is laid out in four wards, or sections, around Independence Square. The Fourth Ward has eighteen sites that are hundreds of years old, including the Old Settlers Cemetery behind the First Presbyterian Church. Some tombstones date from the 1700s. Discovery Place, the city's main attraction, is near Fourth Ward Park. Visitors can see the science museum, aquariums, and even a rain forest with exotic birds and waterfalls. The biggest planetarium in the United States is also in a theater here. After Discovery Place, stop by Wing Haven Gardens and Bird Sanctuary. You'll find more than 135 kinds of birds here, including warblers and mockingbirds.

For basketball fans, Charlotte is home to the Bobcats, an NBA team that was founded in 2004. The Carolina Panthers football team plays at Bank of America Stadium.

There's a lot to see just a short drive from Charlotte, too. The Reed Gold Mine in Stanfield was the first gold mine in the United States. Twelve-year-old Conrad Reed found gold on his family farm here. His discovery set off the first gold rush in the country. About ten miles (16 km) south of Charlotte is a large theme park called Carowinds.

Fans crowd into Charlotte Bobcats Arena to watch their team play basketball.

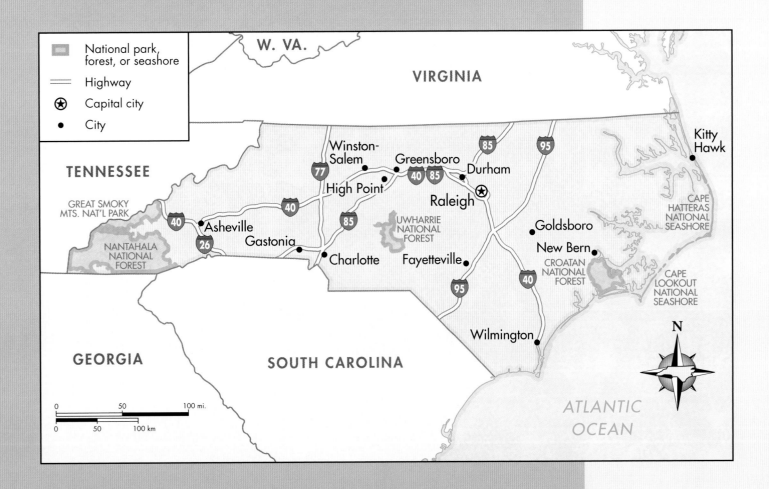

National park, forest, or seashore

Highway

Capital city

City

W. VA.

VIRGINIA

TENNESSEE

GREAT SMOKY
MTS. NAT'L PARK

NANTAHALA
NATIONAL
FOREST

40

26

Asheville

Gastonia

40

77

Winston-
Salem

High Point

85

Charlotte

85

40

85

Greensboro

Durham

Raleigh

UWHARRIE
NATIONAL
FOREST

Fayetteville

95

95

40

Goldsboro

New Bern

CROATAN
NATIONAL
FOREST

Wilmington

Kitty
Hawk

CAPE
HATTERAS
NATIONAL
SEASHORE

CAPE
LOOKOUT
NATIONAL
SEASHORE

N

ATLANTIC
OCEAN

GEORGIA

SOUTH CAROLINA

0        50        100 mi.

0     50     100 km

Take a time-out at
Carowinds theme park!

Take a roller coaster ride standing up on Vortex, or hunt ghosts and collect Scooby snacks in Scooby Doo's haunted mansion. The park also sponsors Education Days, where you can learn about science, math, and more through workshops, demonstrations, and exhibits.

The North Carolina Zoological Park is near Asheboro. It is the country's largest walk-through natural habitat zoo, where the animals and plants are shown in their natural settings. Five miles of trails wind through the Uwharrie Mountains where you'll see gorillas, giraffes, polar bears, tropical birds, and many other animals.

At the North Carolina Zoological Park you can see all kinds of animals in their natural environment.

Other attractions in central North Carolina include the Sandhills in the southeast. It is a popular golf resort, and the area also has a number of peach orchards. About eight miles (13 km) east of Greensboro is the Charlotte Hawkins Brown Memorial State Historic Site. It is located on the campus of a high school for African Americans. Dr. Charlotte Hawkins Brown ran the school for fifty years.

## Western North Carolina

The mountains of North Carolina attract visitors year-round. In the Black Mountains, you can climb Mount Mitchell, the highest peak in the eastern United States. Great Smoky Mountain National Park and other state parks have campsites and hiking trails. You can also visit their craft shops.

The northern mountain region of the state is called the High Country. The town of Blowing Rock in the Blue Ridge Mountains got its name for a good reason. If you toss a lightweight object over the 4,000-foot (1,220-m) cliff at the Johns River Gorge, it may come flying right back to you! Even snow appears to fall upside down. Nearby is Tweetsie Railroad, a railroad that dates back to 1866. If you take a ride on the Tweetsie today you'll see lots of beautiful scenery—but you may also have to

This building is at the top of Mount Mitchell, the highest peak east of the Mississippi.

MOUNT MITCHELL
HIGHEST PEAK EAST
OF MISSISSIPPI RIVER
ELEVATION 6684 FT

**Bascom Lamar Lunsford (1882–1973)** grew up in the mountains of North Carolina. He played the banjo and fiddle and recorded more than 300 local songs. He founded the Mountain Dance and Folk Festival in Asheville.

opposite:
This 250-room house was built for 26-year-old multimillionaire George W. Vanderbilt. Today it is one of North Carolina's most popular tourist sites.

## SPECIAL LANGUAGE

People who live in the Appalachian Mountains speak a special dialect, or a slightly different version of English, called southern mountain dialect. Here are some examples:

| Southern Mountain dialect | Standard English |
| --- | --- |
| *a give-out* | an announcement |
| *hoof* | walk |
| *garden sass* | vegetables |
| *a whoop and a holler* | quite a distance |
| *coon's age* | a long time |

fight off train robbers from the old Wild West!

Asheville is the largest city in the mountains. About 63,000 people live here, including many artists and craftspeople. The Penland School of Crafts is located 45 miles (72 km) northeast of Asheville. It is the oldest and largest arts and crafts school of its kind in North America. Also in Asheville is the Park Place Education, Arts & Science Center, where you can visit several museums and go to the theater all in one spot.

The Biltmore estate, home of George Vanderbilt, is also in Asheville. Vanderbilt was one of the wealthiest men in the United States. With 250 rooms, the Biltmore Estate is the largest private residence in the nation. Some of Vanderbilt's relatives still live here. In 1996 the North Carolina Arboretum opened gardens on part of the estate, with flowers planted in patterns. The Quilt Garden is arranged in the pattern of a country quilt. It took